BETTER THAN BOTH

The Case for Pessimism

Peter Heinegg

Hamilton Books
A member of
The Rowman & Littlefield Publishing Group
Lanham · Boulder · New York · Toronto · Oxford

Copyright © 2005 by
Hamilton Books
4501 Forbes Boulevard
Suite 200
Lanham, Maryland 20706
Hamilton Books Acquisitions Department (301) 459-3366

PO Box 317
Oxford
OX2 9RU, UK

Library of Congress Control Number: 2005930763
ISBN 0-7618-3312-9 (paperback : alk. ppr.)

for Rosie, Max, Alex

And I thought the dead who have already died more fortunate than the living, who are still alive; but better than both is the one who has not yet been, and has not seen the evil deeds that are done under the sun.

—*Ecclesiastes* 4. 2-3

CONTENTS

ACKNOWLEDGMENTS

Thanks to Penguin Books Ltd. for permission to quote from N.K. Sandars' translation of *The Epic of Gilgamesh* (Penguin Classics 1960, Third edition, 1972). Copyright © N.K. Sandars, 1960, 1964, 1972; and to Grove/Atlantic, Inc. for permission to quote from Samuel Beckett, *Waiting for Godot*. Copyright © by Grove Press, 1954. All other translations in the text, unless otherwise indicated, are by the author.

1

AN INTRODUCTION TO PESSIMISM:
WHAT ARE THE ODDS?

Here I, Dionysius, lie, dead at the age of sixty.
Born in Tarsus, I never married; too bad my father did.

—Epitaph from *The Greek Anthology*

Why is it that we rejoice at a birth and grieve at a funeral? It is
because we are not the person involved.

—Mark Twain, *Pudd'nhead Wilson's Calendar* (1894)

There's something ludicrous about being (or being taken for) a
pessimist: the word itself conjures up a long face, humorless tsk-
tsking, and dismaler-than-thou body language. Americans are proverbially
bidden to watch the doughnut, not the hole; and aren't pessimists fixated on
holes? George Santayana may have had a point when he wrote in *Character
and Opinion in the United States* (1920): "American life is a powerful
solvent. It seems to neutralize every intellectual element, however tough
and alien it may be, and to fuse it in the native good will, complacency,
thoughtlessness, and optimism." But then Santayana was born in Spain and
died in Italy—just another decadent Old European. *Real* Americans are
constitutionally incapable of pessimism.

Pessimists are widely taken to be whiny and self-indulgent. One thing
for sure: you need a certain basic degree of comfort and well-being to take

time out for venting your despair over the universe. Nietzsche mocked Schopenhauer, who decried all of existence as a cheat and an illusion, for complacently playing the flute after dinner. People struggling to keep body and soul together, or ducking bullets, generally don't have the leisure for pessimism (and so the suicide rate is higher in Sweden than in Algeria).

To the popular mind pessimism is little more than a permanent bad mood. Pessimists may turn out to be right when they predict that something—the war in Iraq, for example—will come to a bad end. But it's axiomatic in America that negative thinking is at best useless and at worst a self-inflicted wound. Martin Luther King, Jr. famously had a dream; and every politician and immigrant and prospective home-owner in this country has his or hers. Indeed, many patriotic souls would insist that the USA itself is one grand dream come true against all odds (despite a few ongoing glitches). Audiences applaud when the sentimentalized version of Don Quixote known as "the Man of La Mancha" proclaims his resolution to "dream the impossible dream," which would seem by definition a complete waste of time and a guarantee of heartache—but not here.

The logic of optimism, if not its mythical status, is obvious. Hope is fuel for the soul; and while you may not get to your destination, you're going nowhere without it. (Americans blithely misread the story of Pandora's box, as if hope were the only remedy for all earthly evils—ignoring the fact that hope itself is portrayed here as literally the ultimate evil.) By contrast, what could be more self-defeating than pessimism? The power of positive thinking, the little engine that could, "When you walk through a storm, keep your head up high," yadda yadda yadda. Even Virgil (not an especially cheerful poet) said, "Possunt quia posse videntur," they can because they think they can. Where chemotherapy can't stop cancer, redirecting your thoughts might just do the job. Pessimism, it would appear, is a philosophy for losers (and terminal cases).

Precisely. The argument of this book is that life, when all is said and done, is a losing proposition; and to recognize that fact is to be a pessimist. Pessimism might, but doesn't have to, imply depression and misery. If we apply the pragmatist standard that truth is what works, and if it turns out that the world is pretty much as pessimism describes it, then the pessimist would have the most accurate map of reality, and so be least likely to get lost. And not being lost on our journey through life would seem to be an advantage. Sooner or later, delusive notions of where we are and where we're headed are likely to cause problems.

The notion referred to in the title, that being dead is better than being alive, and being unborn is better than both, may sound either contradictorily sour, since Solomon, the supposed author of Ecclesiastes, also said, "Light is sweet, and it is pleasant for the eyes to behold the sun" [11.7]) or simply absurd, since not to have been born can never be an option for any conscious person. As the bumper sticker says, "If you can read this, you're too close"—and it's too late.

Despite all that, the idea appears again and again in world literature, from Sophocles to Heinrich Heine ("Sleep is good, death is better;/ The best, of course, would. be never to have been born"). Perhaps more revealing, however, is the pessimism implicit in Judaism, Christianity and Islam. The great 18th century rabbinical sage, Moses Chaim Luzzato, writes in *The Path of the Just*: "And what man in his senses could ever believe that humans were created for the sake of being in this world? For what is human life in this world? Or who really finds joy or tranquility in this world? 'For the days of our years are threescore and ten; and if by reason of strength they be fourscore years, yet is their strength labor and sorrow; for it is soon cut off, and we fly away' (Ps. 90.10). How many kinds of trouble and sickness, pains and vexations there are. And after all that—death. You will not find one person in a thousand on whom the world lavishes pleasure and true peace and quiet. And if that one person were to reach the age of 100, he soon passes and disappears from the world."

Christians too believe that earthly life is worthless without the afterlife. "If for this life only we have hoped in Christ, we are of all men most to be pitied ... If the dead are not raised, 'Let us eat and drink, for tomorrow we die'" (1 Cor. 15.17,32). And Muhammad keeps reminding his listeners that, "Know ye that this world's life is only a sport, and pastime, and show, and a cause of vainglory among you! And the multiplying of riches and children is like the plants which spring up after rain—Their growth rejoiceth the husbandman; then they wither away, and thou seest them all yellow; then they become stubble" (57:19, tr. J. M. Rodwell). Were it not for the splendors and terrors of Judgment, human life would apparently be no more than a bothersome trifle. But at least a few of the 1.2 billion Muslims on the planet must suspect that the probability of such a day of reckoning is exceedingly dim. And then what?

Naturally, if death ends everything, once dead, the truth of life becomes totally irrelevant to the erstwhile human. Dead believers won't feel indignant over having been cruelly suckered. And the pessimists won't be able to say, "I told you so." But maybe being in the know can be helpful here and now, even as Buddhists praise the value of knowing that "all things are suffering" (a pessimistic axiom, if ever there was one). In its rambling, non-methodical way this book will try to sketch out some features of that help.

The key to its arguments, all of which are more or less old and traditional, is probability. None of them is certain or absolutely irrefutable, just—I maintain—so likely that's it's not worthwhile considering the alternatives except cursorily. Thus, it's barely conceivable that a 63-year-old (my age) golfer will win the next U.S. Open; but no one in his or her right mind would bet on a sexagenarian and against Tiger Woods or anybody in the top ten. A traveler flying to San Francisco in August might bring a raincoat, while another person flying to Mexico City in the same month might not; but both would be stupid, because San Francisco averages zero rainy days in August, while Mexico City averages 27. An openly gay American male could run for President some time soon, but no one in Las Vegas would "like his chances." One could drive at 110 miles an hour from New York to Buffalo on the Thruway and assume one wouldn't be pulled over once in the course of that nearly 500-mile trip—but it wouldn't be a smart assumption.

Of course, philosophical arguments can't be quantified; so all the previous examples limp. But the only real difference between those instances and the issues addressed here is that when it comes to ultimate questions, many people throw away the common sense they apply to less earth-shaking matters. (What is common sense except applying probability to everyday decisions?) In the most pessimistic book in the Bible the author, who disguises himself as Solomon, flatly states: "I said in my heart with regard to the sons of men that God is testing them to show that they are but beasts. For the fate of the sons of men and the fate of the beasts are the sane; as one dies, so dies the other. They all have the same breath, and man has no advantage over the beasts; for all is vanity" (Eccl. 3. 19-20).

Now *there's* an unprovable assertion, if ever there was one. We have no idea what it's like to belong to another species, much less what the non-human experience of death is. But turn on the probability switch and ask anyone who has watched a beloved pet die: Is there any reason to think your own future death will be essentially different from this? Will your post-mortem existence be any different from a cat's or a dog's? Why? This point will be dealt with in more detail later, but the logical answer is intuitively obvious.

To press it just a bit further, what are the "odds" that the concept of "Holy Writ" (a form of expression transcending every human utterance) makes any sense at all? That the world was created by some divine fiat? That Jesus actually rose from the dead? That the world will end in a sublime

"Universal Judgment," akin to the one painted by Michelangelo in the Sistine Chapel? That we can speak meaningfully in the same sentence of the horrors of history and "amazing grace, how sweet the sound"? Gimme a break.

In his "Wager" Blaise Pascal notoriously tried to parlay the chance, however remote, of there being eternal rewards and punishments after death into grounds for a skeptic to "bet" on Christianity. (One in a billion is better than nothing.) Mathematicians have scoffed at this use of probability; and ordinary readers have protested that the amount risked in the "Wager" (all the pleasures forgone by massive and continuous instinctual renunciation until death) is way too high, so that one wonders: did *anyone* ever actually try this?

In any case, probability, if not the only guide to life, is at least the default mode. What this comes down to, most of the time, is not taking needless risks or even bothering to think seriously about the long shots. There's no harm in buying a lottery ticket (if you can afford it); but only maniacs spend hour after hour visualizing what they'll do with the prize money. The philosophical equivalent of that would be optimism, memorably defined by Voltaire's disillusioned Candide as "the madness of claiming that everything is fine, when everything is bad." While that's no doubt over the top, one might recall that the most optimistic American president of the 20th century, Ronald Reagan, proved to be, when it came to the lives of poor and helpless persons, one of the very worst.

If one could live forever in a fool's paradise, then pessimism might be simply a recipe for misery and depression. But we can't (except for perfect fools), and it isn't. And if one lacks the toughness to follow the painful advice of Stein in *Lord Jim*, "In the destructive element immerse," it's still a good idea to learn how to swim in it, as opposed to trusting the leaky water wings of optimism.

One problem with many classic formulations of pessimism is the tendency of certain pessimists to swing for the seats, to make thunderous overstatements, perhaps in frustration at the smugness or simple-mindedness of their opponents. Thus, Jean-Paul Sartre declares in *Nausea* (1938) that, "Every thing in existence is born without reason, goes on living out of weakness, and dies by chance." So much for final causality. But Sartre is ignoring the fact that people (sometimes) deliberately breed plants, animals, and other people. Some living creatures go on living out of gusto or curiosity or even, in the case of humans, because they believe in some grand cosmic scheme. It happens. And a significant minority of human beings plan and effect their own deaths.

Still, Sartre has a point: to stress the random, factitious, accidental features of existence, which are many indeed, and to hassle complacent essentialists. Perhaps he (and all pessimistically inclined thinkers) should have borrowed William James's term, "tough-minded." In *Pragmatism* (1907) James characterizes tough-minded persons as "empiricist, sensationalistic [as opposed to "intellectualistic"], materialistic, pessimistic, irreligious, fatalistic, pluralistic, and skeptical."

Those adjectives pretty much define a thoughtful modern person. By "intellectualistic" James meant someone who proceeds by abstract principles, as opposed to empirical experience. By "fatalistic" he meant anyone who denies free will; and while some pessimists might not want to go that far, it seems pretty clear that the realm of free will, if it exists, covers a very small patch of the human sphere.

So, pessimists and potential pessimists, welcome aboard. As this book hopes to show by reviewing the pessimistic tradition, you're in good company. Oh, and as for the apparently off-the-deep-end idea that (as Yeats translated Sophocles), "Never to have lived is best, ancient writers say:/ Never to have drawn the breath of life, never to have looked into the light of day;/ The second best's a gay goodnight and quickly turn away"—look at it this way: Nobody can speak for the unborn (although it's true that fetuses are often in no hurry to exit the womb and not especially happy once they get pulled out). And no one can speak for the dead either, since the overwhelming majority of them have lived and died anonymously, without leaving behind their "vote." But there's at least a strong possibility that if both groups had seen what would have, or actually did, come their way, most of them would have opted out. Just because they never were and never can be polled doesn't mean it isn't something worth thinking about. Whence this book.

2

BRAIN FEVER:
PSYCHOLOGICAL PESSIMISM

104. *Imagination.* It is the dominant part in man, the mistress of
error and falsehood, and all the more deceitful in that it isn't
always so; because it would be an infallible rule of truth if it were
the infallible rule of lying. But, while false most of the time, it
gives no indication of which it is, marking both true and false
with the same character, ... Imagination disposes of everything.

168. Let everyone examine his thoughts; he will find them all
taken up with the past or the future. We almost never think about
the present; and if we do think about it, it's only to get some light
for managing the future. Thus we never live, but we hope to live;
and while aiming to be happy, we inevitably never are ...

—Pascal, *Pensées* (1670)

The roots of pessimism run everywhere, but perhaps the most
convenient place to start examining them is the human brain, where
everything human begins and ends. In *The Myth of Sisyphus* (1942) Camus
says that the feeling of absurdity arises from tension between the world,
which is *not* absurd, just its ornery self, and the mind, which by a parallel
quirk insists on doing its own contrarian thing—searching for and
(childishly?) demanding rational order, regardless of the fact that it's not
there. If the world actually made sense in some ultimate way, which it
doesn't, or if we gave up trying to make sense of it, which we can't, the
absurd would disappear.

There are, of course, various ways out of this dilemma: most notably the path of religion, which answers all our questions by claiming or pretending that even though we can't know the answers or see the big picture, Someone Else does; and once we are (re-)united with Him, all our troubles will be over. The problem is that positing the existence of a Creator-Redeemer, etc. doesn't necessarily change the experience of death and finiteness or our desire to escape them. Life has a way of feeling much as it did before "we first believed."

On the other hand, we could, in theory, work to convince ourselves that such desires are crazy and "accept the universe" as is. Some people, like Margaret Fuller (and millions of more traditional believers), claimed to have done so (even as Thomas Carlyle foolishly wisecracked, "Gad, she'd better," as if the alternative were unthinkable); and they may well have. (One wonders whether Fuller changed her mind whilst she was drowning in a shipwreck off Fire Island in 1851.) Less consistent thinkers might stop searching for sense and just enjoy or endure the bumpy ride without complaining. But other people can't. Natural selection favors creatures who cling fiercely to life, who aggressively defend themselves, who energetically seek to satisfy their needs. We see this in our pets and other animals; but, unlike us, they don't notice or bemoan the decay of their bodies, nor do they know about death. They do whatever they do easily, unabashedly and unself-consciously. As Walt Whitman said in *Song of Myself*:

> I think I could turn and live with the animals, they are so
>   Placid and self-contain'd.
> I stand and look them long and long.
> They do not sweat and whine about their condition,
> They do not lie awake in the dark and weep for their sins,
> They do not make me sick discussing their duty to God,
> Not one is dissatisfied, not one is demented with the mania
>   Of owning things,
> Not one kneels to one another, nor to his kind that lived
>   Thousands of years ago,
> Not one is respectable or unhappy over the whole earth. (32)

Easy for them, one might object; they have no choice. In any event, it would be nice if humans could live like "happy" animals; but the educated ones, among others, can't seem to manage this. Part of the reason no doubt lies in the old Scholastic adage, "The mind is, in a way, all things"—because it forms an "intentional union" with everything that it can (here comes a heavy-duty metaphor) conceive. Which means that one can, and inevitably does, fantasize about everything under the sun, especially unreachable possibilities. But that in turn guarantees frustration and sorrow. "A man's reach should exceed his grasp," Robert Browning, an enthusiastic Christian, declared, "or what's a heaven for?" Nice try, but it follows that if there's no heaven—something which most thoughtful people would rate a near-certainty—then we're doomed to grope for what can't be had. As my grandmother used to say, our eyes are bigger than our stomachs, whence life's perpetual bellyache.

This is not exactly news. Call most people's attention to the fact that we can only know, experience, or possess the tiniest fraction of the things we might—if we were God, for example—and they'd no doubt reply, "C'est la vie. No big deal." A perfectly logical response, but humans can't stop themselves from feeling shortchanged. Schopenhauer once said that the predominant expression one finds on the faces of older persons is disappointment; and a brief survey of aged shoppers in any supermarket or mall will back him up. Actually, this seems to be less true of traditional societies (the Hmong or Hopis, say, the faces of whose elders often display remarkable dignity and serenity) than of individualistic cultures caught up in the notoriously frustrating "pursuit of happiness."

Then again, disappointment seems inevitable, if only because a) in any given situation one can imagine an endless variety of paths to take, but only one of them can actually be taken at any one time, which perforce excludes all the others; and b) in many cases poverty or some other physical pressure often forces us to trudge along an unwanted path or stay trapped in place.

There are a number of proposed solutions for this problem, most of them stemming from the 19th century, when it became especially urgent (when, for example, the hitherto barely noticed scourge of boredom began to raise its head). In the face of his vanished Christian faith and the cosmic optimism it supported, Thomas Carlyle offered the remedy of frenetic, self-forgetting work ("Produce! Produce!"), which countless millions who never read him seem to have adopted. After his nervous breakdown, John Stuart Mill decided that aiming directly for happiness was guaranteed to fail; happiness could be achieved only as a by-product of striving to promote the common good. Charles Baudelaire, before his awful death from syphilis in 1867, recommended constant "drunkenness" (on wine, poetry, or whatever). Still later, the ever-restless and unhappy Leo Tolstoy would preach living for others, though he never quite found the knack of doing this himself. "Since we are always planning how to be happy," Pascal said, "it is inevitable that we should never be so."

Perhaps the oldest and the most philosophically consistent attempt to solve the difficulties caused by the insatiable ego has been the Hindu-Buddhist attack on it as an insubstantial fabrication. "You who are slaves of the self and toil in its service from morning till night, you who live in constant fear of ... old age, sickness, and death, receive the good tidings that your cruel master does not exist. Self is an error, an illusion, a dram. Open your eyes and wake up" (Paul Carus, *The Gospel of Buddhism*, 1894).

This makes sense—or at any rate much more sense than the typically Christian assault on the self as diseased and hopelessly corrupt—but one wonders how many people, apart from monks and other adepts, have ever pulled it off. Since, for good or for ill, love (desire) makes the world go round, it's hard to imagine more than a tiny minority of humans permanently escaping the tidal pull of samsara and thus swimming beyond the reach of pessimism.

In the final analysis, there are a myriad reasons why despite its logical and emotional force, pessimism doesn't prevail, not consciously anyhow, in the hearts and minds of most men and women. Life brings a nearly infinite supply of distractions (both pains and pleasures will do), deceptions, and the million things that crowd our days' agenda.

For various reasons, including busyness and self-deception, we rarely bother to take time out and "do the math," adding up the pros and cons of human life—an admittedly complicated assignment. But if we did, using a sufficiently broad data base and judging as impartially as possible, we'd undoubtedly come up with a pessimistic conclusion, or at least some serious doubts that the game was worth the candle. But by then we'd be, as we are now, too caught up in the game to stop. And if we accept the statistical likelihood of frustration, pain, and futility, we can always imagine winning the Power Ball lottery, being the one in 200,000,000 or whatever persons who dodges the snares and snags all the prizes. Pessimism can't change this foolhardiness (though age and experience often dampen its glow); it simply advises us—assuming we're not prepared to embrace either monastic life or suicide—to grin and bear it. We can deal with Camus' absurdist view of the mind-world conflict by saying, "So what else is new?"

That doesn't quite solve the problem. In *Nathan the Wise* (1779) Gotthold Emmanuel Lessing memorably said, "Mocking your chains doesn't make you free" (IV, 4); but it at least offers some relief. And since the only way to break completely free from the chains of the human condition is to commit suicide, most of us will settle for a pessimistic jab or two.

The Buddhist claim that the self is an illusion is stronger medicine than most of us are willing to take. The "dear self," as Kant called it, seems at first blush the most obvious and intimate thing in the world; but ask a few questions, and it begins, if not exactly to disintegrate, at least to start breaking down. And that may serve the case for pessimism by undermining the naïve certitude of optimists, religious and otherwise, who are so intent on self-fulfillment in one way or another.

In his *Treatise of Human Nature* (1739-40) David Hume writes: "When I enter intimately into what I call myself, I always stumble on some particular perception or other, of heat or cold, light or shade, love or hatred, pain or pleasure. I never can catch myself at any time without a perception, and never can observe anything but the perception. When my perceptions are removed for any time, as by sound sleep, so long am I insensible of myself."

So what exactly is your self? The face shown on your driver's license, passport, obituary or mugshot? Some mysterious focus of energy commanding a larger network of systems, like a pilot in the cockpit of a 747? Or is it like a pebble thrown into a pond, generating and encompassing concentric circles: body-clothes-house-possessions-family-friends-society-images of ourselves in other people's minds, etc.? Is the self just a linguistic convenience, a subject of sentences? Can a self exist without words? (Apparently not.)

The questions and problems never cease: where is the self when we sleep? (Temporarily gone, Hume argues.) Where is the past self? the future self? And, of course, the big one: what happens to the self when we die? (No one, as Lucretius and many others have observed, seems to care about where the self was, or how it was doing, before we were born.)

The self appears enormous from within, but we know it's fantastically small and insignificant. One long look into a clear night sky is enough to show us *that*—even more when we learn how the view translates into numbers. The Buddha, one imagines, would have loved modern astronomy, would have enjoyed Terence Dickinson's *Nightwatch: A Practical Guise to Viewing the Universe* (1998), where we learn that the earth, a microscopic fleck of cosmic dust, weighs 6 billion trillion tons, that the solar system is bound by gravity to a "permanent family" of galaxies located in a neighborhood spanning three million light-years.—But at this point imagination fails completely, if it hasn't failed before, because few human beings travel more than a handful of light-seconds in their whole lives. Three million light years simply doesn't register—and besides, that staggering distance applies just to the "Local Group of Galaxies," itself a mere .00000003% of the entire universe. Measured against all that, one human body, the fragile container and precious sacrament of the self, disappears. Size matters.

Or maybe not. Perhaps all that "soulless material" somehow pales before the splendor of the conscious self. Perhaps consciousness or the self defies quantification. That's something many of us like to believe, for instance when we say that life (a self) is priceless. In any event when we rope it in with birth and death dates, height, weight, and other facts and figures, its grandeur dwindles. Our *little* life is rounded with a sleep. What will be left of *any* self in a million years (a blip on the screen of *das All*)? Mayflies or Methusaleh, there isn't much difference. The more we learn about the world, the more realize how close we are to being practically nothing. Buddha couldn't have been more right.

Except for one thing (which he knew): it doesn't feel that way. We have no real awareness of cosmic time; as far as our sensorium is concerned, we have always been here and always will be. David Hume (whose insights Buddha would have welcomed too) said that we know the self only as shaped and altered by some "particular perception." To be is to feel this or that; and what for convenience' sake we may call a self keeps getting flooded with sensations. One can train oneself to dismiss them intellectually, to control them, to meditate on their nothingness. One can deaden oneself to the pain and pleasure they cause, but one can't make them go away, except by anesthesia or death. Buddhists quarrel over the precise nature of nirvana; but the word itself means "snuffing out," and it doesn't seem a gross distortion to view it as extinguishing the hot flame of our perceptions.

That's an interesting idea, and quite possibly the sanest of solutions to humanity's troubles, but not a viable short-term option for people raised in the self-centered, self-promoting, self-pitying culture of the West. We don't have, or want to have, the stuff of kamikaze pilots, Islamic suicide bombers, Hindu fakirs, or even Buddhist monks and nuns. We are fed with and get drunk on the myths of individuality, of making a name for ourselves, of stuffing the self in every way: with wealth, fame, sex, power and influence, fans and followers. The men (they are almost always men) with the biggest selves get to be called giants; and, whatever else they do, they dwarf the rest of us.

But *every* self, tiny or enormous, cries out for satisfaction, moans in pain, yawns in boredom, roars in rage or enthusiasm: a booming chorus that even the wisest and most serene Buddhist would (does) have trouble quelling. Judaism and Christianity stress the right ordering of the heart as the key to the good life; Buddhism wants to have us screw our heads on straight. What to do?

In the end we have to plot our course with the best information available (even if we slow down or stop, hoping for clearer signals, the current of time will sweep us irresistibly along), which means science. And science, for example cosmology, seems to be saying: look at the big picture, where you're next to nothing. This perspective runs counter to what traditional religion and secular humanism have long told us: that we are the "crown of creation," the monarchs of all we survey, and stuff like that. All the sciences—all forms of knowledge, including the arts—open up abysses of incalculable size and complexity in which we can lose our selves, to our great advantage.

But not completely. Even if we plunge into an "O altitudo" (the handy Latin word meaning both height and depth), we almost always bob to the surface: me again. On that, sense perception has the last word, and every perception has a nametag and an owner. Still, he or she can vary greatly in size; and a lot of evidence suggests that here too the bigger they come, the harder they fall. The smaller the I, the fainter the ouch. Pessimism advises a discreet irony, a self-deflating sense of humor in thinking of and dealing with the "center of the universe," our precious self, a delicate bubble that won't bear much probing. Be what you are, a tiny, momentary, accidental collocation of atoms en route from who-knows-where to who-knows-whither, a biological field of force just about to fold, fade, and disappear. So, if you can't be a consistent Buddhist, you might as well be a pessimist. Pessimism fits the facts.

3

CHAINED TO THE SLAUGHTER-BENCH:
HISTORICAL PESSIMISM

One intellectual excitement has, however, been denied me. Men
wiser and more learned than I have discerned in history a plot, a
rhythm, a predetermined pattern. These harmonies are concealed
from me. I can see only one emergency following upon another
as wave follows upon wave, only one great fact with respect to
which, since it is unique, there can be no generalizations, only
one safe rule for the historian: that he should recognize in the
development of human destinies the play of the contingent and
the unforeseen.

—H.A.L. Fisher, *History of Europe* (1935)

History … is indeed little more than the register of the crimes,
follies, and misfortunes of mankind.

—Edward Gibbon, *Decline and Fall of the Roman
Empire* (1776-1788)

The word "history" began with Herodotus' modest term meaning
"inquiries," but nowadays most people think of history as "social
science." This is more than a little dubious, especially given the gigantic
gaps of information from ancient times and the unmanageable mountains
of data and conflicting perspectives generated by modern times. If history
embraces all that has been recorded and remembered of human doings, then
there is obviously no way to get a handle on it (not to mention the baffling

abyss of "pre-history"). One can at best take a certain number of "soundings," and argue on the basis of them.

Nonetheless, along with dizzying proliferation of statistics has also come a hitherto unavailable detailed overview of many parts of the world. And it is probably fair to say that the news these data bring us is not good. Consider the following more or less randomly chosen item of "current events," an excerpt from "Planet of Slums" by Mike Davis (*New Left Review* 26, March-April, 2004), which draws on information from the U.N.:

> There were about 924 million slum dwellers in 2001: nearly equal to the population of the world when the young Engels first ventured onto the mean streets of Manchester. Indeed residents of slums constitute a staggering 78.2 percent of the urban population of the least developed countries and fully a third of the global urban population.

Davis cites a U.N. reporter's findings about Lagos State, two- thirds of whose 3,577 square miles could described as slums]:

> Unlit highways run past canyons of smouldering garbage, before giving way to dirt streets weaving through 200 slums, their sewers running with raw waste. So much of the city is mystery. No one even knows for sure the size of the population—officially it is 6 million, but most experts estimate it at 10 million—let alone the number of murders each year [or] the rate of HIV infection.

Whether or not the "smouldering garbage" of Lagos ever bursts forth into a conflagration of terrorism even more devastating than the present one (2004), the lives of countless anonymous human beings have already been destroyed or poisoned; and one can only wonder at all the imponderables raised by this "situation." E.g., assuming that the total quantity of human misery has never been higher than it is today (with more sufferers than ever), how does its quality compare with that of the eons of unremitting pain and suffering in the past? Hasn't even a modicum of comfort and security always been unattainable for the majority of people? Will this ever change? How much of this misery can be attributed to sins of commission or omission by the rich?

In the Bible God needed only ten generations before deciding that the world, or the human part of it at least, was a great big mistake; so he drowned everyone and everything drownable except for the passengers on Noah's ark. Afterwards, shocked perhaps by his own violent overreaction or at least recognizing that humanity was incorrigible, he promised never to flood it again.

Naturally, that left him with many other Doomsday scenarios; and the genre known as apocalyptic, found in both Testaments, describes with psychedelic images and sadistic relish how God, overwhelmed once again by the suffering of the just and the misdeeds of the powerful, belatedly finishes the job. This is good news for the "righteous" (presumably a minority), but a dreadful, in fact an eternal, disaster for their tormentors (often collectively labeled "Babylon").

In any event, apocalyptic writings assume that the world as we know it is a lost cause; heaven or the afterlife or the Kingdom of God or whatever name the Grand Finale goes by is somewhere far, far away from here. Perhaps there'll be a totally transfigured planet earth, but still nothing we'd ever feel familiar with ("And night shall be no more; they need no light of lamp or sun," says Rev. 22.5). The earth as we know it is, it seems, beyond redemption.

Well, there's a lot of good historical evidence for *that* depressing summary, although even the most brilliant cliometrician would find it impossible to supply a single formula for evaluating all of human history. In *Gulliver's Travels* (1726), despite his tiny guest's attempt to disguise the truth, the King of Brobdingnag (rightly, to Swift's mind) reaches a radically pessimistic conclusion about public events in England: "He was perfectly astonished with the historical account I gave him of our affairs during the last century [the 17th], protesting it was only a heap of conspiracies, rebellions, murders, massacres, revolutions, banishments, the very worst that avarice, faction, hypocrisy, perfidiousness, cruelty, rage, madness, hatred, envy, lust, malice, or ambition could produce."

That sort of response is typically written off as evidence of Swift's extreme misanthropy. But what if the King had seen evidence from the 20th century, with its 200-plus million people slaughtered on and off the battlefields? (In passing, it might be noted that the word "misanthrope," like the word "adulterer" or "drug-addict" has only negative connotations. Someone who hates the human race is thought of as ipso facto unbalanced and mean-spirited. On the other hand, to be a philanthropist is automatically good, although only the rich can qualify for the title.)

Meanwhile, at least since the publication of *Candide* (1759) "optimism" has conveyed a certain aura of naiveté, so that people who call themselves optimists often begin by apologizing, ironically, edgily or otherwise, for their willingness to fly in the face of ugly facts. If pressed, most educated persons would admit to being, in one way or another, meliorists, a view that seems to allow for both hopefulness and truth. This is understandable, because acknowledging or admitting the ultimate futility of human life is an unappealing prospect, like having to leave the Super Bowl before half-time because the game is so desperately lop-sided.

But meliorism, in principle, allows for fiercely negative estimates of the past. And then, given such a wretched starting point, the prospect of things improving might not offer much consolation, especially if that improvement came every so slowly. Consider the impassioned cry of William Morris (1834-1896) in *Art and Socialism*

> I say that we of the rich and well-to-do classes are daily doing in like wise unconsciously, or half-consciously it may be, we gather wealth by trading on the hard necessity of our fellows, and then we give driblets of it away to those of them who in some way or other cry out loudest to us. Our poor laws, our hospitals, our charities, organized or unorganized, are but tubs thrown to the whale [i.e., a token gesture to avert disaster]; blackmail paid to lame-foot justice, that she may not hobble after us too fast.
>
> When will the time come when honest and clear-seeing men will grow sick of all this chaos of waste, this robbing Peter to pay Paul, which is the essence of Commercial war? When shall we band together to replace the system whose motto is 'The devil take the hindmost' with a system whose motto shall be really and without qualification 'One for all and all for one'?
>
> Who knows but the time may be at hand, but that we now living may see the beginning of that end which shall extinguish luxury and poverty? When the upper, middle, and lower classes shall have melted into one class living contentedly a simple and happy life?

When indeed? One can't imagine that if Morris were brought back to life today and made to watch or day or so of CNN (despite the countless ways it and the other American media sugarcoat the bitter truth), he'd find much to congratulate us on.

Along these lines, another way to measure history would be from the prospective of its beleaguered, oppressed majority: women. Most feminists would charge, and most rational people would have to admit, that all human societies to date have mistreated women, and that all still do to a greater or lesser extent. If late 20th century demographers could point to the 100 million missing women, how many girls were killed or allowed to die in previous ages before they could be counted? Every society in the history of the world has trampled on the rights of woman; and there's no country on the planet where women enjoy complete equality with men. In the two biggest countries in the world, China and India, gender ratios are now disproportional because of all the female fetuses that have been aborted and the baby girls who have been allowed to die in favor of precious males.

On the basis of patchy improvements and token liberations, many observers (e.g., female college students in the USA) seem inclined to believe that the worst is over, and the old nightmares are gone for good. (Of course, the spread of fundamentalist Islam might suggest otherwise.) But, again, if we closed the book of history right now, the misery inflicted on women would have to be seen as overtopping any modest advances.

And what about the poor, who have always been in the majority, perhaps never more so than now? At least a billion people in the world go chronically hungry, and no one can count the numbers of those lacking adequate clothes, shelter, education, and medical care—surely it's the majority of earthlings. Slavery has always been part of the human condition, and it still is. One estimate puts the number of slaves in the year 2000 at 26 million.) Ignoring for the moment the thousand natural shocks that flesh is heir to, what about the infinite number of gratuitous shocks administered by humans (most of them men) to children, aliens ("foreigners," "infidels," etc.) workers, the sick, the handicapped, the vulnerable)?

One of the familiar ironies about this endless cycle of cruelty is that in describing it, both writers and ordinary folk often have recourse to animal metaphors (as in *King Lear*), while humans notoriously exceed all other creatures in intra-specific violence—and in violence to every other member of what Aldo Leopold called the "biotic community." How often is human behavior "humane"?

Despite his own worshipful histories of "great men," the generally gloomy Thomas Carlyle said, "Happy the people whose annals are blank in history books!" (*Life of Frederick the Great* [1865] IV, 3). But even the generally comic James Joyce had his stand-in, Stephen Dedalus, say in *Ulysses* (1922) that, "History is a nightmare from which I am trying to awake." That sounds like an abstract, highfalutin statement from an artist-intellectual, which it was, in the sense that you'd have to know a great deal before you could have such a nightmare to begin with. Nevertheless, it's interesting that many religions (including Marxism) have a built-in pessimism, whether or not their adherents explicitly recognize it.

Jews long for the Messiah because the world has so often been such a dreadful place for their kind. Christians and Muslims focus on the end of the world because, even though they may not have been personally persecuted as the authors of Revelation and the Qur'an were, they see villainy triumphant on earth. Marxism is supposedly optimistic with its utopian vision of the disappearance of history in the bad old sense, but not because it sees much that is positive in the past. (And now, of course, most Marxists have given up the fight. The future, it turns out, didn't work after all.)

The more one thinks of it, the only way to get any kind of positive grasp on history is through blind faith. As Hegel, who wasn't a pessimist, said: "What experience and history teach is this—that people and governments never have learned anything from history, or acted on principles deduced from it" (*Philosophy of History*, 1832). That sounds like a wild generalization; but even if it were false (and don't generals always prepare for the last war?), it's hard to avoid the impression that humankind staggers from one sort of mistake or catastrophe to another sort, with no net improvement.

For example, after the monstrous self-inflicted wound of the Civil War, it might seem unlikely that the US would ever repeat that particular kind of horror. But whatever "wisdom" was learned from the Civil War (and could any lesson be worth *that* still not-fully-paid price?), it didn't prevent the lunacy of the Spanish-American War (and the succeeding butchery in the Philippines), the US entrance into World War I (which only helped to start World War II and the Holocaust), the Vietnam War, and so forth. The Armenian genocide didn't prevent the Jewish genocide, which didn't prevent the Tutsi genocide, etc. Insane criminalization of alcohol in the 1920s didn't prevent insane criminalization of psychotropic drugs for the rest of the 20th century and beyond.

The historical record, then, as unmanageably enormous as it is, seems to provide the strongest single pillar in the case for pessimism. Now that we've grown suspicious of permanent essences ("human nature") and abstract definitions (humans made in "God's image," etc.), it strikes most of us as fair to say, "The human race *is* its history." That history has been a more or less non-stop succession of an almost uniquely human activity: war. Unfortunately, those who know best the awfulness of the human race are unable to talk about it, because they are beyond speech: the dead and the animals. This round, then, has to go the pessimists.

The only possible argument against them would be a hopeful evocation of the future. But what reason is there, really, to think that the future will be anything but more or the same, patched up here and there? Oy vey. And with that spontaneous cry one is willy-nilly carried back to reflect on the ultimate historical horror: the Holocaust, which gives the lie, now and forever, to optimism. At this point I can't pretend to have anything new to say on the subject, but the following summary conclusions may be appropriate here:

1) To begin with, all the quarrels over the uniqueness of the Holocaust strike me as futile. I readily accept the crude definition by the woman, whoever she was, who simply called the Holocaust "the worst thing that ever happened." Some writers want to give it a kind of sacred status as an ineffable mystery, which makes limited sense. (Such critics might well dismiss my effort to see "lessons" in the Holocaust as a naive trivialization.) But the Holocaust ultimately has a place on the vast continuum of evil that it shares with the other horrors of the 20th century and before, from Turkey to Rwanda. And we *can* talk about it, even though the term "Holocaust," as has often been pointed out, is utterly inappropriate. How could genocide be a "burnt offering"? To whom? "Sanctifying the Name"? (*kiddush ha-shem*, the traditional phrase for martyrdom). What did God have to do with it? Better the cold plainness of Shoah or Hurban, but these have yet to become common parlance in English and doubtless never will.

Whenever I do talk and think about it, I find myself reeling from one aspect of the Holocaust to another: from the sheer numbers of the slain (one hopes that Raul Hilberg's original "low" estimate of 5.1 million is right) to the grisly variety of the forms of death (deliberately fomented starvation, exhaustion and disease; hanging, shooting, burning and gassing; elaborate torture and summary execution) to the incomprehensible madness of slaughtering people instead of just pragmatically robbing and enslaving them, to the cold-blooded bureaucratization of monstrous procedures (as opposed to eruptions of blind hatred), to the massive contribution by hundreds of thousands of "Hitler's willing executioners" (not just Germans, but Austrians, Lithuanians, Latvians, Ukrainians, Poles, Hungarians, Slovaks, Frenchmen, etc. etc.), to the way the destruction consumed not just people, but culture, language, and every material and spiritual feature of the past while spawning a hideous new culture and language (the *Lingua Tertii Imperii* dissected by Viktor Klemperer in 1975).

All of these things were horrible enough in themselves, but when fused into a whole, linked in a sort of row of scythed chariots, they reduced the spectator to helpless grief and rage. The world after the Holocaust had henceforth to be defined as the sort of place in which these sorts of things could always happen. *Ab esse ad posse valet illatio*, as the medieval schoolmen used to say. Anything that has happened can happen.

2) Grisly as all the stories were, from the *Einsatzgruppen* in 1941, to the Wannsee Conference in 1942 (four days before I was born), to the liquidation of the Warsaw Ghetto in 1943, to the annihilation of the Hungarian Jews (which claimed my wife's aunt and other relatives) in 1944,

the death marches in 1945 (when the war had long been obviously lost), they didn't tell the worst: the survivors' (or liberators' or narrators') perspective always skewed things too positively. They could never tell first-hand about the excruciating final moment when the Nazis triumphed, of how it felt when the bullet blasted through the back of the neck or when the Zyklon B pellets turned to gas and the agony of asphyxiation began. People talked a lot about Auschwitz (where my great-uncle died, among the million-plus others), but that was because it was actually the more "benign" part of a death camp, whereas the pure death camps of Treblinka, Sobibor, Belzhets, Chelmno and Majdanek were swallowed up in obscurity. Most of the witnesses to murder there had been murdered themselves. Few people visited them, and there was little to see at the sites now greened over.

But wasn't this typical? The worst moments of the worst terrors and torments in history had always gone unrecorded: the countless thousands of slaves and rebels crucified by the Romans, the Aztec prisoners butchered by the myriads (Inga Clendinnen pointedly reminds us of them in *Reading the Holocaust*), the Africans who died on the Middle Passage, the victims of Stalin and Mao and Pol Pot. There were no scribes writing, no cameras rolling when *they* were swallowed up in the black hole. And then there was the banal, but indisputable, fact that here, as elsewhere in the intermittent Hell of history, what all but a tiny handful of the perpetrators of the Holocaust had in common was, not their anti-Semitism, their Christian roots or their cruelty, but their testosterone. They were all, God damn them, men.

3) The Holocaust definitively abrogated the covenant between God and his people. Not that God hadn't failed to keep his word in the countless pogroms and persecutions before then; but this was the limit. Jews (and Christians) often claimed that memory was redemptive (liturgical practice, among other things, was based on that notion). Not this time: the "sacred history" (*Heilsgeschichte*, from Abraham to the rebirth of Israel) that theologians liked to talk about had been replaced by suffering-history (*Leidensgeschichte*, from the Jewish War to the 1946 pogrom in Kielce, and beyond)—but without the aesthetic comforts of tragedy.

It was a grim fulfillment of the scenes in *The Trial* where Joseph K. keeps finding childishly lettered signs or cheap pornography or stupid faked portraits, instead of the beautifully inscribed Torah he is looking for—a scrawl, not a scroll. Of course, the notion that God had ever chosen a people (for no particular reason, judging from Genesis) and then watched over its destiny, punishing here, rewarding there, macro- and micro- managing everything behind the scenes, was never more than an ingenious conceit, perhaps even an obnoxious delusion. But it was pleasant to entertain it; and there *was* something quasi-miraculous about the stubborn survival of the Jews. Well, that was by the board. As Itsik Manger said, *"Nor mir di galitsiener mekhn dikh oyf eybik oys,/ fun der eyde emese oyeve-yisroel"* ("But we the Galicians forever exclude you [God] from the congregation of the true lovers of Israel.") In some poems about the Holocaust God was needed, if only to pour abuse on.

4) In a broader sense the Holocaust put paid to all the genial anthropo-morphic visions of a world where there was some grand Judge in charge and some sort of long-term justice. Of course, we didn't need the Holocaust to realize this. The notion that one had to wait for the Holocaust to abandon traditional theism would have made Voltaire and Freud, among others, smile ruefully. But again the Holocaust was the clearest, most vivid demonstration of God's impotence. All Jeremiah's and Job's and Qoheleth's complaints, it now turned out, barely scratched the surface. "Behold, the tears of the oppressed, and they had no one to comfort them." There wasn't even delayed justice, as the great majority of Nazi criminals went unpunished and died in their beds.

5) Throughout all this, one undeniable fact about the Holocaust was its power to fascinate. If ever there was such a thing as the pornography of violence, this was it. As a stunning set of limit-situations, where human experience was pushed to every conceivable extreme, it turned us all into rubber-neckers, like motorists passing a spectacular chain-collision. Fifty years later, the questions still burned: what would you have done if you were … (a Jew ordered to dig your own grave before the "nape-shot"? a member of a *Judenrat*? part of a *Sonderkommando* at a death camp? a sympathetic gentile in Poland? a would-be assassin of Reinhard Heydrich? FDR?) No use pretending, teaching all this, as I did in a course on Holocaust literature was infinitely more *interesting* than Milton's theology or *Le Cid* or Romantic alienation or the poetry of W.B. Yeats. Where else in the world could one find so astonishing (and weirdly comic) a tale as this one, reported in Martin Gilbert's *The Holocaust* (pp. 200-01), about a survivor of an Einsatzgruppe massacre in Ejszsyski, Lithuania, the sixteen-year-old Zvi Michalowksi, who had fallen a fraction of a second before the volley of shots which killed those next to him, including his father. Later he had heard the chief executioner, a Lithuanian named Ostrovakas, singing with his fellow executioners as they drank to their successful work.

Just beyond the Jewish cemetery were a number of Christian homes. Michalowski knew them all. Naked, covered with blood, he knocked on the first door [wait, was this a fairy tale? PH]. The door opened. A peasant ... was holding a lamp which he had looted earlier in the day from a Jewish home. "Please let me in," Zvi pleaded. The peasant lifted the lamp and examined the boy closely. "Jew, go back to the grave where you belong!" he shouted at Zvi, and slammed the door in his face. Zvi knocked on other doors, but the response was the same.

Near the forest lived a widow whom Michalowski also knew. He decided to knock on her door. The old widow opened the door. She was holding in her hand a small burning piece of wood. "Let me in!" begged Michalowski, "Jew, go back to the grave at the old cemetery!" She chased him away with the burning piece of wood as if exorcising an evil spirit.

Michalowski, desperate for shelter, returned. "I am your Lord, Jesus Christ," he said, "I came down from the cross. Look at me—the blood, the pain, the suffering of the innocent. Let me in." The widow crossed herself and fell at his bloodstained feet. "Boze moj, Boze moj," "My God, my God," she kept crossing herself and praying. The door was opened. Michalowski walked in. He promised the widow that he would bless her children, her farm, and her, but only if she would keep his visit a secret, and not reveal it to a living soul, not even the priest. She gave Michalowski food and clothing, and warm water to wash himself. Before leaving the house three days later, he once more reminded her that the Lord's visit must remain a secret, because of His special mission on earth.

This being a miracle story, Michalowski went on to join the partisans and survive the war. The exception proved the rule. The Holocaust, as Lucy Dawidowicz said, was the war against the Jews; and in many crucial ways the Nazis won.

Apart from personal accounts there were also the films: the old U.S. Army newsreels of the German concentration camps they (or the British) liberated in the spring of 1945. It was hideous and jolting, especially the scenes from Bergen-Belsen, with piles of corpses being bulldozed into a giant pit. Actually, compared with the unfilmed scenes from the death camps, it was little enough Sooner or later one thought of that quasi-documentary, *Schindler's List*, whose credits end with the camera lingering on the rain-soaked road, built of tombstones from a desecrated Jewish cemetery, through the Plaszow work camp once ruled by Amon Goeth. That might serve as closure, of an obvious, visual sort (actually, the headstones themselves had to be manufactured for the film). But if the Holocaust had taught me anything, it was that no closure with it was possible, not for my generation. As seen in the suicides of Paul Celan (1970) and Primo Levi

(1987) or the mother of the creator of *Maus,* Art Spiegelman (1968), the damage done couldn't be healed, even long afterwards. It could only fade, not vanish, an asymptote never reaching oblivion. Like all of life, the Holocaust was first transient and then immutable. There could be reparations (though seldom paid and mostly a pathetic symbol); but there was no redemption, nor would there ever be any. History was and is beyond redemption. To read it was to become a pessimist.

4

NOT A PRETTY PICTURE: PESSIMISM AND OLD AGE

Youth is a blunder; Manhood a struggle; Old Age a regret.

—Benjamin Disraeli, *Coningsby* (1844)

Practically, the old have no very important advice to give to the young, their own experience has been so partial, and their lives have been such miserable failures.

—Henry David Thoreau, *Walden* (1850)

Take the sum of human achievement in action, in science, in art, in literature—subtract the work of the men above forty, and while we should miss great treasures, even priceless treasures, we would practically be where we are today ... The effective, moving, vitalizing work of the world is done between the ages of twenty-five and forty.

—William Osler, *Life of Sir William Osler* (1925)

Middle-aged and old people often complain about the way TV and the movies are monopolized by the cult of youth: twenty-some-thing characters, with smooth faces, lustrous hair and perfect bodies, a never-ending stream of kids who seem to get younger even as the nation gets older, and centenarians become the fastest-growing chunk of the population. Cable news shows are "anchored" by mostly blond, exquisitely coiffed cuties. Older stars on sitcoms or detective shows have to be flanked, if not surrounded, by sexy male and female assistants half their age, regardless of the improbably youthful and model-quality surgeons, lawyers, and lab scientists this winds up creating. Even actors touting such geriatric products as Centrum Silver, Depends or, God help us, funeral homes are a decade or two younger than their target audience. Most strikingly for older viewers, TV shows are awash, partly no doubt out of political correctness, with glamorous young female professionals, quite in line with the percentages of women now in medical or law school, but hardly with the numbers of the movers-and-shakers already installed in boardrooms and executive suites. At least television doesn't pretend, not yet, that there are lots of stay-at-home dads, or any male receptionists in doctors' or dentists' offices, or that the President is going to be a woman any time soon.

In any case, if the motivation of the complainers is obvious, so is that of the producers: we all want to look at splendid human specimens, not decrepit geezers. Old people's life-stories are mostly over. They have few meaningful, much less dramatic, choices to make, sexual, professional, or otherwise, apart from drawing up their wills. They're unlikely to change, except for the worse, as they drift downward into death. After a while they don't even make convincing criminals. And then there are the laws of the market place: young consumers have decades of buying power ahead of them; advertisers have to grab them now. So, absurd as it may be (and what weird notions Martians who knew America only from TV would have about our demography), youth will continue to reign over the media, even as the old (-ish) actually hold the reins of power.

No big novelty here. In the long run, perhaps the only serious drawback with all this is that the preternaturally young, firm-fleshed casts of TV shows (especially in that oxymoronic genre, "reality TV") also include such a vast majority of numbingly tedious airheads, of no particular ethnicity (that *they* can remember), with no discernible history or politics or causes or anything to talk about except their own inconsequential feelings and so-called "relationships."

These are all commonplaces, but they have a perhaps overlooked corollary: long before MTV, *Vogue, Rolling Stone, Friends* or *American Idol*, before the launching of the non-stop parade of dewy pop icons, much of the world's great art, music, and cultural achievement came, and continues to come, from the hands of fairly (or very) young creators, who were at the height of their physical and mental powers. And so their work, even when dark or tragic, inevitably contains, or betrays, the boundless energy—and vitalistic bias—of youth.

Not that there haven't been great masterpieces produced in the autumn or winter of the artist's life. Sophocles' *Oedipus at Colonus*, composed when its author was nearing ninety, presumably wins first prize in this category. Three cheers for the work of Titian (who died at 99), Frank Lloyd Wright (90), Michelangelo (89), and Tolstoy (82). And there have been, of course, splendid tragic treatments of old age from Homer's Priam in Book XXIV of the *Iliad* to Shakespeare's Lear to Rembrandt's self-portraits to Flaubert's Félicité in *A Simple Heart*. But in classical literature the *senex*, the silly old fool, is the stock comic figure; and he has continued to be.

Old men are killjoys; they want to marry their luscious young daughters to geeky or repulsive or downright wicked suitors. They're stuck in their ways; they're slow-moving, dull-witted, and sexually impotent (just ask Boccaccio). They blather and potter around. They just don't get it. Nowadays, thanks to Viagra and "quality medical care," such dotards may have more of a future than their coevals once did, but it's still pretty pathetic.

Once again the caricatures—not to mention true-life portrayals—of old age make plenty of sense. As Hamlet twitted Polonius (himself an exemplary blend of senile ridiculousness and clueless malice): "The satirical rogue says here, that old men have gray beards; that their faces are wrinkled; their eyes purging thick amber and plum-tree gum; and they have a plentiful lack of wit, together with most weak hams" (II, ii, 197-201). Come to think of it, the great bulk of the dramatis personae in Shake-speare's plays, except some of the histories, are made up of the young. In *Much Ado About Nothing*, for example, only Leonato and Antonio *have* to be over thirty-five. Shakespeare, who died on his 52nd birthday, presumably would have echoed Sir William Osler's conviction of "the uselessness of men above sixty years of age."

The examples of youthful predominance could be multiplied ad infinitum. Novels, from Richardson to Dostoyevsky, from Fielding to Stendhal, from Defoe to Proust, Kafka, and Joyce are mostly about young people, their adventures and disasters. And how not? For most of the history of painting and sculpture, artists, from Botticelli to Modigliani, have shown us young, if not deliciously beautiful, bodies. Men and women in nursing homes don't moonlight as models (or anything else).

Music is a field where, like sports and math and physics but unlike philosophy or politics, you don't necessarily have to grow up before you reach the heights. Consider the achievement of Henry Purcell (died at 36), Mozart (36), Juan Crisóstomo Arriaga (19), Schubert (31), Mendelssohn (38), Chopin (39), Bizet (36), Schumann (went insane at 44), Gershwin

(38), the Beatles and the bulk of jazz and rock musicians, from Bix Beiderbecke (28) to Jimmy Hendrix (28).

As for poets cut off in their prime, the list is far too long to cite, from Catullus (30) to Hart Crane (33). Here are some obvious choices: Chatterton (17), André Chenier (32), Keats (25), Shelley (30), Byron (36), Pushkin (38), Lermontov (27), Rimbaud (stopped writing poetry at 19), Mayakovsky (37), Wilfred Owen (25), and so on. One doesn't have to wait till "full maturity" (whenever *that* may come) to achieve greatness. "In my early years," Dr. Johnson told Boswell, "I read very hard. It is a sad reflection, but a true one, that I knew almost as much at eighteen as I do now" (i.e., 1763, when Johnson was 54, a venerable age back then).

In fact, not surprisingly, Shakespeare wrote *Hamlet* in his late thirties, Beethoven wrote his *Eroica* symphony in his early thirties. Joyce finished *Ulysses* in *his* late thirties. The "problem" is that such exuberant productions from the pen of geniuses at the peak of their powers represent spectacularly privileged moments of human experience—which is why we keep returning to them. But they hardly recreate the texture of day-to-day life as lived by ordinary mortals, much less the gradual dilapidation and dissolution of old age or even the awkward, blotchy unripeness of adolescence (which, except for some NBA draftees, seems to grow longer and longer in modern culture). As Nietzsche said in *Human, All Too human* (published in 1878, when he was only 34), "Art makes the sight of life bearable by drawing over it the veil of fuzzy thinking."

If art were a mirror of life or simply "true to life," we would scarcely need it. Compare the complete, complex reality of a great city, Rome for instance, with the idealized, abstracted presentation of it in a Michelin guide, with its crisp, Cartesian list of one-to-three star attractions and carefully focused highlights: the vast stretches of banal, ugly, dirty, wretched living space encompassed by the real Rome (the shoddy postwar housing, etc.) never make it into the book and are ignored as far as possible by the tourist. What percentage of "bestsellers," much less ordinary published books, ever gains admission to the canon? Art goes for the cream of the cream, hence its appeal.

Stendhal said the beautiful was a "promise of happiness." That promise is always kept, at least insofar as aesthetic experience goes. (Thomas Aquinas defines the beautiful as "that which pleases when seen," and pleasure is certainly happiness. But what if one wanted that pleasure in a more pragmatic sense? What if, à la Pygmalion, one fell in love with an idealized nude? (All classical nudes are idealized.) None of the various enthralling female (or male) characters in art is "available." Nietzsche roundly mocked Kant for saying that the beautiful is "what pleases us without interest," as if the aesthetician had to abandon anything so crude as desire for real objects in the real world.

That makes sense, of course, but it simply confirms the old pessimistic conclusion that art is (much) better than life: art tells coherent stories with beginnings, middles, and ends (never found, strictly speaking, on planet earth). It raises human conversation to impossible levels of cohesion and eloquence, eliminating all the aimless noise and boring banter we actually hear and engage in. (One of the best versions of idealized speech is the rat-a-tat-tat of taut, muscular stichomythia, whether in Greek tragedy or on cop and doctor shows, where the characters neatly exchange rapid-fire jolts of incredibly dense information.)

This idealization reaches a blissful quasi-eternal state, as Keats, that supreme youngster, kept telling us, in the peak-experiences of art. We have to make art and refresh ourselves with its eternal youth because otherwise we'd be stuck forever in the quotidian rut. How many ordinary lifetimes would one have to go through before hearing an ordinary person spontaneously burst into an aria from *The Magic Flute*? So all art is at once and forever good news and bad news. It brings joy along with a reminder of how rare joy is. (How often do our spontaneous sentences rhyme? How often do our scribbles turn into calligraphy?)

And the message of pessimism here is, as always: savor the passing pleasure, but don't mistake the gorgeous dreams of art for the real "big picture." The Hallelujah Chorus resounds in concert halls, not within any non-existent Pearly Gates. Battle-scarred, balding, fiftyish husbands and their mistresses in motel rooms do not—ever—talk like the fiftyish Mark Antony and the 38-year-old Cleopatra whom Shakespeare imagined. The Classical Antiquity created by the Renaissance can never actually be "reached," in the sense that anybody with enough cash in hand can reach Heathrow Airport.

One of the paradoxical results of the idealizing nature of art is that it communicates delight even when its message is bleak. Kafka and Beckett, for instance, keep returning to a ludicrously awful and impossible world, which we nonetheless take pleasure in and applaud, because art, including the art that expresses desolation, creates elegant, ingenious, witty formal structures (remember the old "school figures" in ice-skating and the fussy judges who used to measure them with calipers?); and we can't help liking it. But it only provides temporary asylum—and asylum from time—not, as Scripture says, a lasting city.

All pessimism asks is that we include the non-idealized realities of life—for which old age, with its concomitant wrinkles, sagging flesh, shrinking muscles, hair loss, impotence, mental fog, and general repulsiveness, can stand as a convenient, if not inevitable, emblem—in our worldview. Philosophically, vast numbers of people seem to be like Prince Siddhartha before he went on his fateful wanderings outside the protected enclave of his palace and discovered (i.e., took seriously) sickness, old age, and death. No one expects to see a three-hour prime-time special—or opera, musical, epic poem, sit-com, or cartoon series—about the final stages of Alzheimer's, ALS, or Huntington's chorea, any more than veterinarians advertise their euthanizing "facilities," or undertakers invite us to tour their basements. Imagine if newspaper obituaries printed, not twenty-year-old photos of the deceased in their prime, but actual deathbed pictures of ghastly, wasted bodies. We have plenty of cuddly shots of naked babies fresh from the delivery room, but none of naked grandpas and grandmas en route to the embalmer or cremator. But when you block all this from your consciousness (as in the media's sanitized war coverage) you radically falsify the truth. And truth is what pessimism is all about.

5

WHAT HAS GOD DONE FOR YOU LATELY? ATHEISTIC/AGNOSTIC PESSIMISM

The doctrine of the Fall claims that God called a weak, sinful race into being out of nothingness in order to subject it to endless torment. And then finally to top it all off, the God who insists on indulgence and forgiveness of every sin, and even bids us love our enemies, does nothing of this himself, but lapses into the very opposite; because a punishment that comes in at the end of the world is of no use either for improvement or deterrence. Thus it is mere revenge.

—Arthur Schopenhauer, *Parerga and Parlipomena* (1851)

Pessimism is often associated with atheism, although it certainly needn't be. Many unbelievers (Thoreau, Robert Owen, Lenin) have been optimists, and many believers (St. Peter Damiani, Calvin, Kierkegaard) deeply pessimistic. The dogma of original sin (which sees all humans as deserving, and many, if not most, of them as actually receiving, eternal punishment) is certainly one of the most pessimistic ideas ever to dawn on anyone. But pessimism is generally linked with godlessness. Dostoyevsky said in *The Brothers Karamazov* that, "If there is no God, all things are permitted," which sounds like the starter's gun in a race toward moral monstrosity. Indeed, the horrors of the 20th century are often viewed as a logical consequence of the denial of God, with the godless trio of

Hitler, Stalin, and Mao duking it out for lethal supremacy. (Alternately, Crusaders and jihadists of various stripes are cited as evidence of the murderous capacities of believers.) For the pessimist all such theological judgments are nonsensical: the human beast will do his thing (and the worst beasts are all men) with or without God; and appeals to, or invocations of, God turn out to be thinly or thickly disguised rants of individual or corporate egoism.

In any case, the argument is often made that unless there is a Divine Lawgiver and Punisher/Rewarder, we're all in very big trouble or at least a wind-tunnel of ethical confusion. On the other hand, atheists like Sartre have insisted that if you want freedom, you have to get rid of God. When Nietzsche said that God was dead, he meant that uppity humans had killed him, i.e., had (with good reason) destroyed something they themselves had created in he first place. True, Nietzsche also added that humans were a long way from appreciating the world-historical implications of deicide. Many casual atheists, it seems, hadn't "grown into" their stupendous crime.

Without making the obviously doomed attempt to reach finality on this question, we can settle for some pedestrian—and ultimately pessimistic—reflections upon the problems of having or not having a God. Perhaps surprisingly for those who haven't looked into it, the "cash value" (as William James might say) of God is in some ways rather limited.

In the Old Testament God, in theory, grants prosperity to his faithful followers during, but not after, their life on this earth, which ends forever with their being "gathered to their people." Of course, if they *aren't* faithful in keeping his 613 commandments, as the Israelites so often weren't, then his punishments could be ferocious. At all events, apart from a tiny handful of scattered and disputed references, there is no mention of life after death in the Old Testament. Later Judaism and, most especially, its wildly popular offshoots, Christianity and Islam, made much of the afterlife, which they saw as providing a permanent answer to the problem of the constant gross miscarriages of justice in our world, as well as satisfying the wish to escape the miseries and frustrations of life on earth.

So far, so good. But in many versions of Christianity and all throughout the Qur'an we find brutally pessimistic accounts of what will happen to most of the human race (and in some readings, even to most soi-disant Christians) at the Last Judgment. As it turned out, the topography and imagery of hell were developed (or, in Dante's case, borrowed) in much greater and more powerful detail than those of heaven. Varying estimates have been made over the centuries as to the population of either place (Purgatory, if it exists, is only a temporary state); and some optimists

(Universalists) have gone so far as to say that in the end everyone will be saved (but the Scriptural basis for such smiley-faced optimism is shaky at best).

Whatever the truth, there can be little doubt that fear of hell has played a larger role in the lives of believers than hope of heaven. Heaven is by definition beyond our imagining—whence the endlessly quoted, "What no eye has seen, nor ear heard, nor the heart of man conceived, what God has prepared for those who love him" [1 Cor. 2.9])—whereas hell, if it hasn't already arrived here on earth, e.g., in the form of famines or tsunamis, is simply an amplification of experiences all of us have had, seen or read about. So the existence of an afterlife, if it plays any role in this life, can best be described as a negative force. And Hell, as unbelievers like Schopenhauer never tire of pointing out, puts God in a very bad light. (Dante didn't flinch at this: his famous sign at the entrance to hell reads: "Divine Power made me, Supreme Wisdom, and Primordial Love" [i.e., the Trinity]). God, it develops, had no choice but to torture his wicked children forever.

Modern Christian theologians seem to have realized how problematic this is; and beyond the intellectual bogs of fundamentalism these days one has to travel a long way to hear an old fashioned sermon on hell, like the one that terrified James Joyce in *A Portrait of the Artist as a Young Man* (1916), and which Joyce himself largely borrowed from Ignatius Loyola's *Spiritual Exercises* (1542). The whole thing is so palpably Baroque-preposterous, as if magnifying anthropomorphic images to the nth power would somehow make them more real.

If it's hard to do a cost/benefit analysis of believing in God when comes to the Beyond ("exit interviews" with dying believers suggest that they're more frightened than consoled by the prospect of Eternity), it becomes well nigh impossible to do so for the here and now. Some people claim to have found love, comfort, and companionship in God, others a steady supply of guilt, fear and depression. Perhaps the larger truth is that humans have no immediate experience whatever of God (to whom, as La Rochefoucauld might say, they would have never given a thought if they hadn't happened to read or hear about "him"), but only of the religious community that worships him. In its cultic life what Émile Durkheim in *The Elementary Structures of Religious Life* (1912) loosely labeled a "church" celebrates itself as impinged upon by the deity. ("God has spoken to us through the prophet," etc.) This could be viewed either as corporate narcissism or as an appropriate response to fantastically good news. Inevitably "churches" use different nomenclatures to divide the world into "us" and "everyone else."

In either case, the direct experience of God is limited to the "professional" inspired seer, who has no other authority for his message than his (this is a males-only club) own conviction. God himself need not be an essential focus of the services "in his honor." In some ways, the less we think about him, the better; because all sorts of unanswerable questions arise (or have been raised since the time of Socrates), such as: We need God because we are, for one reason or another, helpless without him; but why does God need or even want our praise and attention? (If he does need or want them, he sounds like a flattery-addict; if he doesn't, why bother with him?) Are things right or wrong simply because God said so (in which case morality is irrational), or did he say so because they were right or wrong independently of his dictates (in which case God is unnecessary for ethics)?

But if we do decide to get involved with God in person, so to speak, the problems proliferate. How do you/can you deal with a "person" ("somebody" at least somewhat like us) who is at the same time "totally other" (not like us)? How not to feel crushed and overwhelmed by "him"? How to answer Nietzsche's objection in *Thus Spoke Zarathustra* (1883-89) "*If* there were gods, how could I bear not being a God?" Was God simply lucky to be "born divine," with ichor and not blood in his veins, as it were?

The inevitable anthropocentric metaphor calls us God's "children," but that proves to be contradictory and weird, apart from its vulnerability to Freud's accusation (in *The Future of an Illusion,* 1927) that religion infantilizes believers. Among other things, children grow up and become adults; eventually they have to care for their helpless parents and in the end replace them. Perpetual childhood is not a happy prospect. But all the other metaphors used in theology, as we'll see later on, turn out to be equally defective. God as lover? Lovers are equal. God as shepherd? Shepherds raise their sheep for the slaughterhouse. God as king? Royalty is obsolete and intolerable. And so on.

One of the more peculiar features of "relations" with God is the oft-described "dark night of the soul," where God breaks off contact with the believer and leaves him or her in "desolation." A well-known account of this can be found in the "Terrible Sonnets" of Gerard Manley Hopkins:

> I wake and feel the fell of dark, not day.
> What hours, O what black hours we have spent
> This night! What sights you, heart, saw; ways you went!
>
> And more must, in yet longer light's delay.

With witness I speak this. But where I say
Hours I mean years, mean life! And my lament
Is cries countless, cries like dead letters sent
To dearest him that lives alas! away.

I am gall, I am heartburn. God's most deep decree
Bitter would have me taste; my taste was me;
Bones built in me, flesh filled, blood brimmed the curse.

Selfyeast of spirit a dull dough sours. I see
The lost are like this, and their scourge to be
As I am mine, their sweating selves; but worse.

Hopkins apparently suffered from this condition until he died (in 1889), some four years after writing "I wake and feel," although ideally this sense of abandonment is supposed to ease with time. Spiritual writers who treat the "dark night of the soul" ignore the most likely explanation for it: that, like many physical pains and bodily malfunctions, it derives from some sort of unhealthy habit. Change your way of life, and the pain will disappear. Putting it another way, desolation could be seen as the universe's friendly advice to the believer to give up. When the post office returns your letters stamped "No longer at this address," you logically conclude your friend has left.

But, despite the devastating case that has piled up against God (both from keen-eyed unbelievers and from delirious theists like John Donne, Jonathan Edwards and Pope John Paul II), the divinity, some kind of divinity, can rightly be viewed as a last-ditch defense against pessimism. If nothing else, a Creator-Redeemer could serve as a sort of flimsy wall of sandbags thrown up against the rushing torrent of life's threats and injuries. Pessimism warns us that this wall *looks* rather dubious since it disdains empirical proof (beyond that, all a priori arguments about whether God exists, and if so, what we can know about him, always prove futile), and that we should act and plan accordingly. The major reason why the wall is so weak is that everything the prophets, priests and theologians tell us about God crumbles when you lay a logical hand upon it. God may dwell in a realm beyond logic, but we do not.

A perfect example of this is Schopenhauer's objection to the Last Judgment. Everyone knows that earthly life leaves a lot to be desired when it comes to justice; so the invention of a celestial assizes where things finally get straightened out has a strong appeal; and many cultures have enjoyed imagining this. Still, the notion of eternal punishment/reward is utterly crazy (the notion of eternal *anything*—except forever-changing matter—is unthinkable). What would the criteria be? The "cut-off point"? What good would it do to torment the wicked forever? What would life in any "heavenly realm" be like? And so forth. (For more on this theme see the following chapter.)

The fundamentalist-literalist response to such questions ("Scripture says …") isn't worth considering (much of what Scripture says, such as lists, genealogies, and ritual prescriptions is completely irrelevant today). The liberal-demythologized response ("Well, it's all just metaphors …") sounds more intellectually credible, but, in the end, is just as empty (what's left once the metaphors are stripped away?) We are a) trapped in anthropomorphic, anthropocentric fantasies (if we insist on trying to transcend our brain-bound world), and b) those fantasies don't, ultimately, work. As ever, pessimism bids us: Get over it.

Perhaps these theoretical reflections can be translated into a scene familiar to Americans abroad: the hordes of tourists, mostly young, some in shorts and sleeveless tops (not long ago scowling vergers would have stopped them at the door), traipsing through European cathedrals with knapsacks, fanny packs, dangling cameras, and solemn awed-but-bored faces. Refreshed by the cool air (if it's summertime), dwarfed by the soaring arches and sky-high ceilings of the two-to-three star sacred attraction, trying to make some sense of the high altar, the elaborately carved and railed choir stalls, the countless ill-lit and barred side-chapels, with their baffling profusion of (generally) mediocre sculptures, oil paintings, reliquaries, or partially preserved corpses of saints. Some of the visitors con their guidebooks, peer at plaques affixed to the walls, or stare mutely at Latin inscriptions, but there's no mistaking their puzzlement: what to make of this bizarre *Gesamtkunstwerk*, the jumbled product of as many as six to ten centuries and the amalgam of a dozen different styles, from severe Romanesque to treacley 19th century devotional?

Judging from facial expressions and anecdotal evidence, the great majority of these visitors lack any coherent notion of what they're seeing (a few years ago I watched a group of Japanese tourists wolfing down ice cream cones during evensong at Westminster Abbey). Do they even know what the word "cathedral" means? On the other hand, many of them probably do have a clear enough sense of what they're visiting: a tomb.

For one thing, all the sacred persons depicted—in frescoes, mosaics, paintings, carvings, etc.—have long been dead. Though theoretically alive and well and flourishing in some faraway, invisible supernatural realm, they (Jesus, especially, but many later martyrs too) are often shown either dead or dying from horrible wounds and torture. Even Mary, who, we are told, never actually died—since her immaculate conception exempted her from the consequences of original sin, including death, she merely "fell asleep" (whence the feast of her "Dormition" on Aug. 15)—is often shown pierced with swords (an expansion on Simeon's prophecy in Lk. 2.35). Christians believe that death is the portal to everlasting life, but as depicted in Christian art it practically never looks or feels that way.

Sometimes masses will be in progress while the tourist hosts invade: clusters of the aging faithful in a cordoned-off section of kneelers, like little boats at anchor on the bare, stony ocean of the cathedral floor, will occasionally exchange scornful glances with the tourists. The worshipers remind us that the churches aren't yet museums (though nowadays admission is sometimes charged in places like St. Paul's Cathedral in London or the Cathedral-Mosque of Córdoba), but they're on the way to becoming that.

On special occasions, of course, certain cathedrals will be thronged with pious enthusiasts (a papal mass in St. Peter's, for instance). But the prevailing impression is still of an elaborate, mostly deserted marble tomb. The air is cool, damp and melancholy; there are innumerable dignitaries and aristocrats buried beneath the flagstones (part of an afterlife insurance policy: the closer your grave to the tabernacle, the better).

And it's more than an impression: the purpose of all those side-altars, big and little, was to accommodate the vast numbers (now greatly reduced) of priests who used them to a) offer the "sacrifice" of the mass, and b) consume the eucharistic meal of transubstantiated wine and wheaten wafer. The sacrifice was/is a mystical reenactment of the bloody execution of Jesus on Calvary, and the meal is a sublime form of cannibalism. But by now centuries of repeating these weird rituals have drained them of their power to shock—or excite or persuade.

If most of the vacationing visitors can't grasp the historical details (who *was* the martyred St. Vincent—roasted on a gridiron by the Romans—whose bony arm is venerated in the cathedral of Valencia?) and arcane symbolism (what to make of Moses' brazen serpent?) of all the images surrounding them, most of the worshipers have only the foggiest sense of what the cosmic theological drama being performed in front of them by a graying, mumbling priest is supposed to mean.

The world—the human race, at least—is sacramentally (which means both symbolically and actually) redeemed every time a mass is "celebrated." No one knows how many millions of times this has happened, but has it *worked*? Judging from the demeanor of both participants and spectators (not to mention the world outside), it hasn't. No surprise there, since two millennia of Christianity have likewise failed to produce much evidence of salvation.

But at least there's the beauty and solemnity of the site: cathedrals are often the most imposing buildings in any given European city. This combination of beauty and futility creates a tension that Nietzsche remarked on in *Human, All Too Human* (220): "One has to admit, but not without deep pain, that in their highest flights the artists of all ages have raised to a heavenly transfiguration precisely those ideas that we now recognize to be false: they are the glorifiers of the religious and philosophical errors of the human race, and they couldn't have been this without belief in the absolute truth of those same errors. If belief in this sort of truth declines on the whole […] that genre of art can never blossom again which like the *Divina Commedia*, the paintings of Raphael, the frescoes of Michelangelo, and the Gothic cathedrals, presuppose not just a cosmic, but also a metaphysical meaning in the objects of art."

On the one hand, the "Universal Judgment" in the Sistine Chapel is breathtaking; on the other hand (assuming Michelangelo took his subject seriously), it's childishly mythical. Part of being a rational grownup is perceiving how small a place humans have in the scheme of things; and the idea that a tall, heavy-set male, his loins covered by a swirling garment, should be judging the entire world and its history is clearly absurd.

The more recent the church building and the art it contains, the more keen one's sense of absurdity tends to be. Ancient basilicas and Christian sarcophagi take us back to a world where mythical thinking was the coin of the realm. Modern attempts to imitate them—St. Patrick's Cathedral and St. John the Divine in New York, or, God help us, the Crystal Cathedral in Garden Grove, California—seem pathetic (mannered, make-believe, faux) because, one thinks, the architects and artists really should have known (or subconsciously did know) better, known that they were building tombs rather than residences. People who still think it possible that God has "pitched his tent" (Jn. 1.14) among us are welcome to proceed to the nearest cathedral and see for themselves. Pessimists can appreciate the aesthetic value, if any, of the building and its contents. And, unlike a lot of the bored or boisterous tourists, they know enough to show respect to the dead.

In fact, they could even take an imaginative leap and express some sympathy for the much-abused Judeo-Christian-Muslim God, who might well be tempted by all the horrors his "followers" have wrought to imitate Thoreau's famous disclaimer in *Resistance to Civil Government*: "'Know all men by these presents that I, Henry Thoreau, do not wish to be regarded as a member of any incorporated society which I have not joined.' ... If I had known how to name them, I should have signed off in detail from all the societies which I never signed on to; but that I did not know where to find a complete list." And so, rather than ending the history of theism with a Nietzschean "God is dead," we might end it with God's indignant departure, along the following lines:

I

Hello, a message for Hezbollah:
God here, still reigning in Valhalla
(Assama, Paradise, whatever—
Olympus, Heaven—well, I never
much cared what folks called my address)
I've had a fine time, I'll confess,
for lo, these many thousand years,
observing your poor "vale of tears"
(a kaffir term for planet earth),
your non-stop troubles, right from birth.
It *has* been fun, I can't demur:
a lively show with (some *longueurs*),
which really should be no surprise
because, although they improvise,
I *made* the actors (clueless kids,
whose only prompter is their ids),
I sketched the script, I wrote the score,
the scary end, and much, much more.

And so I get a lot of ink—
I'm flattered; pious humans think
so highly of me: hymns and prayers
and pleas for help in their affairs.
I see believers as my fans;
they're all agog about my "plans"
(but now I simply let things roll
this way or that, without control);
and being such a cynosure
has had a certain droll allure.

It's made me blink their odd behavior,
like hailing me as "Lord" and "Savior,"
like dreaming, after lives of toil
and shuffling off their mortal coil,

I'd spare them from their "cruel fate"
and sweep them up to my Estate,
as if I'd want their company
(egad!) for all eternity.

At any rate, I've been amused
by all their crazy, weird, confused,
religious doings—up till now:
their holy books and holy chow
(kashrut, halal, quaint Brahmin rules),
those priests and mullahs (holy fools),
those prophets babbling to the mob
(high time they got an honest job),
those holy places bathed in blood,
Crusades and other sacred crud,
jihads, etc. This may sound gruff,
but here's the word: I've had ENOUGH.

II

I know some folks will disagree:
"It's all a tribute meant for *Thee*,"
they'll prate. Too bad. I hereby quit
my post as "God." Yes, this is it.
Remove my name from church marquees,
from Bibles, Qur'ans, from decrees
by ranting, bearded lunatics,
from preachers'-pastors'-rabbis' shticks,
from shpiels by monks or ayatollahs.
And, by the way, all you Hezbollahs,
you're *not* my party, never were.
I *have* no party, *don't* concur
with God-drunk kamikaze killers;
I don't have troops, much less guerrillas.
I'm sick of humans, frankly bored
with all their cries about "the LORD."
I hereby disassociate
myself from every single statement, shout,* or song by anyone,

---

* E.g., "Allah-hu akbar," "God Bless America," etc.

who lifts his finger/points his gun
and claims that he has heard from me
or shares in my authority.
So (need I say it any louder?)
Allah herewith now takes a powder.

III

Meantime, I'm handing over all
the earth, which I once held in thrall,
to Satan, long my interim
front-office rep. Just turn to him
with orders, bids, requests, complaints.
He has a special corps of "saints"
whose management has been quite steady
(you may have noticed that already).
You should feel free to pour abuse
on *his* head, now that I've cut loose,
or praise him and invoke his name.
He loves that "we're God's party" game;
his finger's deep in all the pies
(how fitting for "Lord of the Flies.")
He *does* love titles (*entre nous*,
he's really just a parvenu)
and all the pomps and perks that go
with being earth's new C.E.O.
Good riddance: for this God-damned gig
no salary could be too big.

IV

Hence, many thanks to H.D.T.,
a non-theistic chap, but he's
the one who got me thinking: "Hey,
why not just ditch this damned *métier*?"
Since, willy-nilly, you're defined
by whatever disgusting kind
of macho theomaniacs
(bin Ladens) wielding Allah's axe
or Yahweh's, e.g., Joshua,
or Christ's (thugs brandishing *la Croix*)
who swipe your name to bless their fight
(how's that for breach of copyright?)
I therefore choose to disappear:

I AM WHO AM is out of here.

    So please accept my resignation
I mean, my sovereign abdication;
or don't accept it: I don't care,
The God Show's going off the air.
I much prefer my solitude
where junk-mail (worship) can't intrude,
where I won't feel the slightest pain
when mortals take my name in vain,
and where at last I can be free
to taste for all eternity,
untroubled by the human race,
the emptiness of silent space.

6

CRUMBLING ROCK OF AGES: PESSIMISM AND THE RELIGIOUS IMAGINATION

Pessimism steps in when religion stumbles badly or collapses completely. This chapter will look at four areas where traditional Christianity (and theism in its usual modes) has experienced a major imaginative failure. Whatever else God is or can be, he serves as a desperate excuse for not taking all the grim evidence about life in this world as the last word. But once the various sloppy theistic pictures of the supernatural break down, optimism is in big trouble.

A. Empty Heavens

Heaven, n. The place of bliss and happiness where God will manifest His glory to all who are saved and where they will see God; the place and state of perfect happiness. Where it is, is not known, except that it is outside of and beyond the earth.

—*A Concise Catholic Dictionary* (1944)

Of all the problems faced by the religious imagination, constructing an even faintly believable picture of the afterlife may be one of the most daunting. The Hebrew Bible leaves the problem untouched, because during the centuries when most of it was composed (1000-160 BCE?), there *was* no belief, or only a flickering one, in an afterlife. The New Testament is fairly restrained on the subject, till we get to the Book of Revelation, which explodes with all sorts of images of the Beyond. This is continued by the Qur'an's naively sensuous vision of Paradise and Hell, but that's a problem for Islamists. The Middle Ages, as everyone knows, talked and wrote and sang about heaven endlessly. Since the rise of the modern science heaven has become increasingly dubious.

The first great hurdle to be gotten over (apart from the primitive, pre-Copernican triple-decker model of the universe seen in almost all visions of heaven, and the inevitable blunt question, "Where exactly is this place?") is the status of heaven's human inhabitants. Paradise exists to reward the good, who first have to be separated from the wicked. But how could that be done? The New Testament imagines this process as similar to a herds-man's separating sheep from goats (Mt. 25.32-33), to farm hands' separating wheat from weeds (Mt. 13.40), and to fishermen's separating good fish from bad (useless) ones (Mt. 13.47-50). But this plainly would not work with human beings.

Even assuming that humans *are* ultimately responsible for their actions (always? how much? at what point?), and that upon their deaths they could be assigned some definitive moral score by some infallible judge (the Celestial Testing Service?) capable of evaluating the millions of factors involved, the idea of some absolute "cut-off point," a divine passing grade, is ridiculous. We might all agree on a few individuals as the absolute monsters and villains of history, and a few more as indisputably good; but, beyond that point, the shades of gray thicken into impenetrability. Of course, Universalists, by claiming that everyone gets saved, solve the ratings issue; but it's not clear what they plan to do with the Hitlers, Stalins, Maos, and Pol Pots of this world.

Continuing the mathematical dilemma, the stakes—eternal weal or woe—are so incomprehensibly high that they create an intolerable disproportion between the merits of the just and the demerits of the unjust. If the concept of an afterlife arose, at least in part, out of frustration with the monumental inequities in a world where the wicked often prosper and the good often perish, and where "time and chance happen to them all" (Eccl. 9.11), then the solution of an infinitely long postlude to right the wrongs of the game only makes the inequities worse—far, far worse.

But again, even if we assume that the impossible binary distinction has been made, and that a state of somehow deserved endless bliss has begun, the headaches continue. How are we to imagine our heavenly condition? Paul attempted to head this problem off when he testily wrote, "But some one will ask, 'How are the dead raised? With what kind of body do they come?' You foolish man! What you sow does not come to life unless it dies.

And what you sow is not the body which is to be, but a bare kernel, perhaps of wheat or some other grain" (1 Cor. 15. 35-37). Well, seeds don't really die, they metamorphose; but again let's assume death led us to some wonderful stage of development that, had we but known it, was implicit in our poor fleshly husks all along. Theologians have a name for this state, the "glorified body."

O.k., but what to *do* with our glorified bodies? The answers given have not been very interesting: praising God and enjoying "the beatific vision." The blessed will have bodies, but apparently no bodily functions, since images of messianic banquets and dining on Leviathan-steaks are not meant to be taken literally. Jesus said that there would be no marrying or giving in marriage in the "resurrection" (Mt. 29.30); Muhammad took a directly contrary view, although heavenly "marriage" in the Qur'an seems to be a euphemism for recreational sex. In any case, hypothesizing a body without real bodily activities, as many Christian theologians do, is meaningless. On the other hand, once grant the existence of countless real bodies occupying real space, and preposterous chaos ensues. Heaven provides an indispensable backdrop for *New Yorker* cartoons, but not much above and beyond that.

Yet if space is problem, so is time. There seems to be no history in heaven, no novelty or evolution. The good news, "And death shall be no more, neither shall there be mourning nor crying nor pain any more, for the former things have passed away" (Rev. 21.4) is paradoxically bad news too, because without tensions, contrasts, struggles, etc. the rhythm of life would be as flat as the EEC of a brain-dead person. Time, as we understand it, seems to have ended in heaven.

Once again, it's a good news-bad news situation. Time, as Proust and Beckett, among others, keep telling us, is the source of all our troubles:

POZZO: (*Suddenly furious*) Have you not done tormenting me with your accursed time! It's abominable! When! When! One day he went dumb, one day I went blind, one day we'll go deaf, one day we were born, one day we shall die, the same day, the same second, is that not enough for you? (*Calmer.*) They give birth astride of a grave, the light gleams an instant, then it's night once more.

  —*Waiting for Godot*

On the other hand, it's the only medium we can work in, the continuum without which we can't continue. The sea in Hebrew literature was for the most part a negative symbol of chaotic forces hostile to God, so the author of Revelation simply decrees its disappearance (Rev. 21.1). Unfortunately, the earth as we know it could no more exist without the oceans than a fetus could exist without amniotic fluid.

Heaven, in the end, is just a cry for relief from the woes of life. But once that relief is imaginatively obtained, we draw a blank. The existence of a world-to-come is dictated by needs: emotional (wouldn't it be nice!), moral (justice at last!), and psychological (what, a world without me?!); but the existence of needs, especially such grand ones as these, says nothing about the likelihood of their being met. The fact that we have no special reason for believing in any sort of afterlife is the main problem. But the fact that we can't even come up with coherent images of it beyond the clichés of Christian iconography—the white-robed choirs, the palm-fronds, angels, or dizzying *trompe l'oeil* ascents through swirling clouds of glory—is also a bad sign. And so it's no surprise that actual belief in heaven has faded and left us with just a hopeful "X"—or, as the Romans used to say, *vox et praeterea nihil*, a word and nothing more.

B. Size Matters—Theologically

> "League all your forces, then, ye powers above,
> Join all, and try the omnipotence of Jove.
> Let down our golden everlasting chain
> Whose strong embrace holds heaven, and earth, and main.
> Strive all, of mortal and immortal birth,
> To drag, by this, the Thunderer down to earth.
> Ye strive in vain! If I but stretch this hand,
> I heave the gods, the ocean, and the land;
> I fix the chain to great Olympus' height,
> And the vast world hangs trembling in my sight!
> For such I reign, unbounded and above;
> And such are men, and gods, compared to Jove."
>
> —Homer, *The Iliad,* VIII, 23-34,
> tr. Alexander Pope

Readers of Homer will recall the scene at the beginning of Book VIII where Zeus ("Jove" in Pope's appropriately bombastic rendition) summons the immortals to Olympus and issues a fierce prohibition against interfering in the war and aiding either the Trojans or the Achaeans. To clinch his threats, he challenges all the other Olympian gods to a tug of war, whose outcome he boastfully predicts. This is not one of the Cloud-Gatherer's more appealing moments; and it paradoxically undermines his point. Reducing his supreme power to such crude physical terms makes him sound both coarse and insecure, if not pitiable; and it comes as no surprise that the Olympians more or less blithely ignore his orders for the rest of the epic. So much for omnipotence—since it probably doesn't exist, it's best not to spell it out too clearly.

Something similar seems to happen to the figure of Jesus when Christians exalt him as divine: we see the emergence of a major credibility gap. Jesus the charismatic teacher, dynamic prophet, and brilliant prose-poet are all believable and welcome figures. But Jesus the Master of life and death, the Lord of history, the Judge of all humanity, the omnipotent, omniscient, omnipresent Alpha-and-Omega, Savior-Redeemer-Ruler?—that looks like a stretch for any human being, even a divine one. Blaise Pascal famously has the crucified Jesus telling the believer: "I thought of you in my agony. I shed such-and-such drops of blood for you" (VIII, 553). *Vraiment*? The average adult has about 22 pints of blood in him. If Jesus had tried to shed even a few drops for each and every one of the billions of people in need of redemption, he would very swiftly become exsanguinated, leaving the bulk of the human race high and (literally) dry. If he shed a tear for all his fellow Jews who died in the Holocaust, much less for all the victims of 20th-century genocides—well, no one has that many tears.

This is one of the downsides to having a human redeemer—he's just not big enough. What you gain in familiarity and intimacy, you lose in power. No doubt part of the problem comes from earlier generations having such a straitened view of the world. For centuries Christians, like Jews before them and Muslims after them, had no idea how large the world really was, how many unknown countries and peoples it contained. Still less did they imagine the staggering age and incomprehensible size of the universe, which reduces even the most powerful humans in history to flickering fireflies on a summer night.

Judaism and Islam might seem to be wiser, or at least luckier, in proclaiming their God to be immaterial, and hence beyond all human limitations (and all merely human persons, such as Jesus of Nazareth, although Yahweh and Allah are both, somehow, persons too). Perhaps the most triumphant expression of this comes in Second Isaiah: "For my thought are not your thoughts, neither are your ways my ways, says the LORD, For as the heavens are higher than the earth, so are my ways higher than your ways and my thoughts than your thoughts" (Is. 55.8-9). What, after all, would be the use of a God whose thoughts and ways were no better than ours?

A God who can't be pinned down to any part of space can much more readily wear the mantle of supposed infinitude; but, on closer inspection, all we have here is the difference between a visible speaker at a microphone and the concealed presence and amplified voice of a Wizard of Oz. The God of the Tanakh and the Qur'an turns out to be quite concrete: emphatically male, often a severe and angry one—though with moments of graciousness, an eloquent speaker of his prophet's mother tongue, but just as human as the mortal authors of the Old (and New) Testament and Muhammad. It was obviously impossible for them to put anything into their accounts of God that they didn't already have or know themselves—and hence his interests coincide exactly with theirs. His word is their word (and outsiders had better not alter it). If He (they) managed to say or do anything truly transcendent, by definition we wouldn't understand it. And the God of Moses and Muhammad can end up sounding as bad as Homer's Zeus. The LORD in the Book of Job is a sublime (and sarcastic) bully: "Gird up your loins like a man, I will question you, and you shall declare to me. Where were you when I laid the foundations of the earth? ... Who determined its measurements—surely you know?" (38.4-5). Allah sounds even more aggressive and repellent: "They who treat 'the Book',' and the message with which we have sent our Sent Ones, as a lie, shall know *the truth* hereafter, when the collars shall be on their necks and the chains to drag them into Hell; then in the fire shall they be burned" (40.71, tr. J. M. Rodwell). The idea that an all-powerful Infinite Being has to (or chooses to) pull his punches until some faraway, ever-fading Judgment Day is bound to seem suspicious.

So the sacred texts (cultures in which literacy was rare idolized writing) of the monotheists are caught in a steel-trap dichotomy: either present warm, graspable images of God (e.g., from the Song of Songs) that are so literally down-to-earth that their religious content verges on nil; or head in the direction of "apophatic" theology, which talks about God only by saying what he isn't (in-visible, in-describable, in-comparable, im-mortal, un-fathomable, un-limited, etc.), and thus remains entirely "up in the air." Hence Léon Bloy's wisecrack that Immanuel Kant's God has clean hands—only he doesn't have any hands. If you want a God with hands, you have to accept the fact that two hands can't hold very much.

It's not God's fault: he presumably did the best job he could, but the world proved to be too big and intractable; and the more's the pity.

C. Biblical Metaphors: Ever Dimmer Glimmerings

You shall not make for yourself a graven image, or any likeness of
anything that is in heaven above, or that is in the earth beneath, or that is
in the water under the earth; you shall not bow down to them or serve
them.

—Exodus 20. 4-5

The Bible's ban on graven images is well-intentioned, but ultimately
futile. You can forbid the making of pictures or statues of God; but verbal
images are indispensable, and the Bible itself is full of them. How could it
be otherwise? What you can't picture, at least vaguely, you can neither
think or talk about. Jewish artists may be forbidden to depict יהוה (or even
pronounce "his" name —though the Tetragrammaton itself is an image), but
what to do with all those poetic images of God as a father, warrior, ruler,
husband, vineyard owner, and so forth? They're anchored in the text, and
no less seductive, vivid, and misleading than images anywhere else.

Christianity, of course, has proved far more receptive than Judaism to
images of God. And Christianity is still more closely linked to a certain set
of New Testament metaphors, e.g., Jesus as Lord, Shepherd, Savior,
Redeemer, Messiah, Lamb of God, etc., which Christian art and literature
have not hesitated to exalt, at times to masterful effect. But these metaphors
are both time-bound, subject to the shifts and reversals of human sensibility,
and intrinsically inadequate, since by definition our words and images can
only point to and suggest, not reach or define, the higher reality they seek
to represent.

Let's look at some of these problems. Any metaphor borrowed from the
monarchies of the ancient world is handicapped by the fact that we have,
one hopes, left such barbarism behind. Enlightened countries—including
all those with a majority population of Christians—have by now rejected
any sort of royalty, except a purely decorative-symbolic one. We all agree
that no human being deserves to have exclusive life-and-death powers over
his or her fellows; so kings and lords and masters are out. We point with
contempt or horror to the public worship of tyrants in Stalin's Russia,
Mao's China, Saddam Hussein's Iraq, or Kim Sung Il's Korea. The
Tarquins (7th-6th centuries B.C.) made *rex* a dirty word in the Roman
Republic; and the rest of the world has come to side with the Romans.

And so all those images of God or Christ as the Supreme Leader
(Pantocrator, the bushy-browed, black-bearded Master of the Universe)

have become obsolete. Whatever is intolerable on the human level is intolerable on the divine level, if there is one. Even if God or Christ occupied a place roughly similar to that of a king, we wouldn't be able to use the image because so many bloody, misguided, or incompetent persons have worn crowns for so many centuries. Imagine a German trying to think of Christ as his Führer. (Imagine naming a 21st century ocean liner *Titanic*.) So, to launch out on a series of tentative updatings, instead of Christ the King, how about Christ the Divine Ombudsman?

Speaking of Christ, that title (= the Anointed One = the Messiah) has caused trouble right from the beginning, because for the Jews of Jesus' day, the Messiah was a mighty Warrior. God's people had been oppressed for centuries by Assyrians, Babylonians, Persians, Greeks, and Romans; and they needed someone like Judas Maccabeus or William Tell or Joan of Arc to set them free.

But, once again, this just won't do. *Our* experience of such national liberators, has been sour, and whatever good Castro or Qaddafi or Khomeini may have done, they stayed in power too long. We don't want a cult of the personality, of the Heroic Generalissimo. How about Christ the Lifeguard?

The obscure metaphor of Redeemer is awash with problems and contradictions. Redeem, of course, means to buy back, as in a pawn shop. What sort of transaction are we talking about here? Jesus buys us back—how? from whom? at what price? Theologians have not been shy about offering answers to those questions, but that has only heightened the confusion: redemption is achieved by Jesus' death or through his blood; he bought us back from either the devil or his Father; in the latter case we have God offering himself to God to atone for an offense committed against God. Or something. If Jesus redeemed us, that might suggest that he owns us, though a rich person can redeem slaves and let them go. How about Jesus the Benefactor or Jesus the Philanthropist?

Jesus the Good Shepherd, an image that can be traced back to the Book of Psalms and the Prophets, may seem to be a modern, gentle and positive metaphor; but, the more you think about it, the more dubious it looks. Marie Antoinette with her perfumed flock on the lawns at Le Petit Trianon, or the amorous swains of pastoral poetry, could afford to be tender with their sheep; but sheep-raising is an industry, and its purpose is to exploit animals for human profit. In the end, all sheep are slaughtered for their meat or hides. The Good Shepherd may go out to search for the one that was lost, but he'll ultimately put her in the pick-up truck with all the rest and drive her to the slaughter house—if he doesn't slaughter her himself; and he won't lie awake at night regretting and fretting over it. Both the rise of the ecology movement (often bitterly resisted by farmers) and the spread of agribusiness have made us take a far more negative view of animal husbandry than in ages past. Instead of the Good Shepherd, how about the Divine Pet Owner? That is, in any case, a lot closer to true love.

Jesus is the divine Judge, but that's problematic too. Many of the tasks of ancient judges, especially in penal matters, have been taken over by juries. Besides, in our world judges are often elected (and so removable at the voters' will). From the town court to the Supreme Court, judges always carry some sort of political baggage and ideological bias. Again, we have too many images of all-powerful judges presiding over bloodthirsty kangaroo courts in Russia, China, and other totalitarian countries, to be comfortable with a towering Omnipotent Judge on Doomsday. Why not the Divine Tribune of the People or Pro Bono Lawyer?

A far less power-oriented image would seem to be Jesus as the Lamb of God who takes away the sins of the world, the sacrificial victim, for example in the Book of Revelation. But here too we run into difficulties. This metaphor is rooted in Exodus 12.6-7; 23: "... the whole assembly of the congregation of Israel shall kill their lambs in the evening. Then they shall take some of the blood, and put it on the two doorposts and the lintel of the houses in which they eat them ... and when he sees the blood on the lintel and on the two doorposts, the LORD will pass over the door, and will not allow the destroyer to enter your houses to slay you"—unlike the houses of the Egyptians, whose firstborn sons he will slaughter. The difficulties here are endless, from the use of blood as a magic talisman and panacea to the impossibly brutal image of the Angel of Death—we've seen too many facsimiles of *him* in modern history. So no lambs, if they have to be butchered and if we have to be smeared with their gore. How about a St. Bernard?

The list of metaphors could be extended, from the dove-Holy Spirit (doves are, in fact, quite aggressive) to the Dionysian communion with the flesh and blood of the dying-and-rising god. But all of them fall short in one or more crucial ways. Of course, thoughtful religious people would freely acknowledge this, only to claim that the problem was to be expected, since we can only reach God by faint analogies anyway. What the poets and prophets who wrote the Scriptures were presumably asking us to do was to take the positives implied by their various images and multiply them by some enormous factor, while quietly ignoring the negative.

But in fact these analogies never get us beyond our human world and its limitations. We are still imprisoned in a hall of mirrors trying to peer out through them. We never transcend our experience, we merely refashion it.

Take one more example: God as Israel's jealous husband, infuriated by her "whoring" after other gods (Ezek. 16 and 23, etc.) The spread of feminism has made us reject the deep-rooted sexism in this metaphor, with its inflammatory language, which makes God the owner of his bride, whom the Scriptures frankly degrade and demonize. But before we get indignant at the inveterate woman-bashing, we might be brought up short by the thought that we're being sidetracked by the rotten sexual arrangements of the 6th century BC(E): after all, the image *is* telling us that God and humans are relating like members, however unequal, of the same species; and that seems to be, if nothing else, a daring statement.

But we're still stuck with the fact that the more accessible a metaphor is, and the more comfortable we feel about it, the more thoroughly we're back in our own human backyard, with no sign of transcendence anywhere. Calling God a husband and Israel an adulteress is merely projecting something well-known (however infected with bias) onto the absolutely unknown. We might translate the situation this way: once upon a time a certain group of men, who thought of God as a super-man, imagined that "he" felt about his unfaithful "chosen people" (as if millions of people could be meaningfully and fairly fused into a single female) much as they or men they knew would feel if *their* wives were cheating on them. In other words, God as Cuckold, or perhaps even God-as-remarkably-tolerant-and-forgiving-Cuckold. This will never, ever do.

Religious language, we are forced to conclude, tells us nothing about the world beyond the believer's sensibility, either because no such world exists or because, if it does, we can't reach, much less grasp, it. The Bible's metaphors crumble in our hands. No doubt this is one of the reasons why the Bible itself (contradictorily) forbids us from making any of them ourselves. Qoheleth's repeated lament that all human activity is "vanity and striving after wind" applies as well to the attempt to create enduring religious metaphors. Another round for the pessimists.

D. The Cloudiest Crystal Ball: Catholic Futurology

Twere to consider too curiously, to consider so.

—Hamlet, V.i.195-96

The following is what the Germans call a thought-experiment. It shows what happens to a theological house of cards when, instead of photographing or admiring it, one gives it a few fillips. Start out with two absolute dogmas of the Catholic Church (shared by tens of millions of non-Catholics and even non-Christians) : 1) that a human being is "ensouled" at the moment of conception (as opposed to when the fetus quickens or is born), and 2) that all human beings will be assigned to a place of eternal bliss or torment after death—and then play with them a bit.

While the Church has, if not called off, at least softened, its campaign on "artificial" contraception (the sin of thwarting the creation of an infinitely valuable—Christ died for it—and sacred soul), it has held the line on abortion. This is a politically realistic move, since the overwhelming majority of Catholic couples (and rational people everywhere) practice birth control, while abortion is much rarer; and here the Church can count on the support of contracepting pro-lifers from across the entire Christian spectrum.

But take a close look at the idea of equating conception with animation, and the difficulties, so to speak, prolifer-ate. Consider the post-terrestrial destiny of embryos or fetuses that are miscarried or aborted. Besides, every day millions of fertilized ova are spontaneously expelled from the wombs of women who never even realized that they were, however fleetingly, pregnant. So no one (except God) noticed the arrival or departure of these tiny entities; but they were, according to the Church, primitive, potential persons. And what about the microcephalic and acephalous and other genetic monstrosities that somehow blunder their way into existence? They too have a share in the afterlife, but what sort of share?

There are three traditional answers, all of them problematic, to this question: a) such souls are unbaptized, and so they must be damned. That notion is outrageously cruel, but Augustine and others have argued for it (since there's no salvation outside the Church, and no way to get into the Church except baptism); b) they will be sent to limbo, a sort of air-conditioned Nowhere, neither blissful nor baleful, just stress-free and comfortable. Of course, such creatures were never fully human, or even close to it, anyway; so presumably they won't mind their persistent vegetative state; c) finally, they might be awarded heaven, if only because the other two prospects seem brutally unfair. One objection to this sunny scenario, however, might be: why should they get off so easily when the rest of the human race had to toil and suffer, not to "earn" salvation, since that's a gift no one deserves, but to fight off the threats and lures of eternal damnation. The elect, one assumes, have to engage in all kinds of good behavior, but these "individuals" have no behavior of any kind on their record.

The same problems apply to babies and children who die before the so-called age of reason (often put at seven years). Of course, if they were baptized, possibilities a) and b) disappear: they *have* to go to heaven; it's in their contract, as it were. The most blessed human phenomenon, from this standpoint, might be crib death. But the nagging issues of a "free ride" to salvation remain. For example, murderers of Christian children would have to be viewed, in the long run, as their victims' supreme benefactors. Call it the King Herod paradox. (The Holy Innocents were, admittedly, all Jewish; but the Church has posthumously awarded them the status of Christian martyrs.) And if *all* innocent children go to heaven, then we might have to partly revise our condemnation of the Holocaust, since the Nazis guaranteed their youngest victims a happiness so immense that the short-term unpleasantness of starvation, shooting, or the gas chambers pales into insignificance.

At any event, in all scenarios involving the death of embryos, fetuses, or infants, one has to wonder: what will their final psychic and personal level of development be? Would an omniscient God have to fast-forward all those unlived lives until they reached a point beyond their original unself-conscious, animal condition? And, by the way, what about the trillions of animals who have accompanied, suffered from and with, been tortured and eaten, etc. by, human beings? Do *they* have any place at all in the afterlife?

The consensus seems to be No, perhaps in part because then, all those beguiling "Peaceable Kingdom" paintings by Edward Hicks (d. 1849) aside, the Beyond would be insufferably crowded and noisy; but many believers have found the absence of their pets and other favorite animals unsettling. Balaam's ass? The dog from the Book of Tobit? The wolf of Gubbio? Heaven and hell are the ultimate monocultures.

If we're going to worry about the lowest end of the human spectrum, we might as well confront the issue of the absolutely unborn. At some point in time, the New Testament (echoing the Old) insists, God is going to bring history to a close: the trumpet will sound, the dead will be raised, and the Last Judgment will begin. (And Jesus assures us that there will be no marrying or giving in marriage after that [Lk. 20.35].) But this means that billions and billions of potential souls will be forever excluded from the chance of endless beatitude. All human contests, offers, and lotteries have their deadline; and non-existent latecomers can scarcely complain. But picture an infinitely long queue of unrealized possible persons being waved away by Gabriel, St. Peter, or whomever, and disgruntledly slipping back into the abyss from which they might have emerged. Does heaven have a limited seating capacity? (Of course, putting a cap on the population of hell definitely seems a mercy.)

Apropos of undeveloped lower forms of human life, there's a related difficulty with all the inhabitants of heaven and hell: given our fluid, inconstant, and always-evolving nature, would humans be "frozen" for all eternity at their finest or vilest moments (as so often in Dante's *Inferno*), or what? Such a solution, even if appropriate, would be unimaginable because there is no such thing as stasis in our sublunary experience. Maybe the blessed would get better and better, while the damned would go from bad to worse. Who knows?

Then there are all the severely retarded, autistic, and congenitally brain-damaged "persons." To what extent would have to be "upgraded" when they entered eternity? Once again, since they never acquired or exercised moral responsibility, i.e., were never "tested," they would have the same unearned advantage as the sainted innocents.

The key to all these mystical theorems and logical loop-the-loops is the totally non-empirical phantasm of the soul. Though part of neither sperm nor ovum, it magically leaps into existence, *divino afflante spiritu*, when they join. Physically undetectable, it becomes present in the womb (although in all ordinary "maculate" conceptions it also brings with it the lethal burden of original sin) and is created even if conception occurs in a petri dish. But it's totally absent from the bodies of the most intelligent, active, and beautiful animals.

Simply deny the existence of soul, however, and the still more improbable fantasy that it lives forever; and all the above-mentioned imponderable dilemmas and difficulties vanish into thin air—where they began. A zygote doesn't have a soul, and neither do you or I. There is no eternal spiritual principle residing in any life form; so all questions of what happens to it in some dream-vision future are completely (alas? thank God?) irrelevant.

Pessimism points out all these imaginative failures of Christianity and reminds us that whatever doesn't work in our imagination, even after trying long and hard, can't work anywhere else. Back to the drawing board. Or rather, just erase the whole blackboard, and try something else. Above all, don't dodge the facts (and the odds garnered from them) right before you in the name of some metaphorical shot in the dark.

7

PROMISES, PROMISES:
AMERICAN PESSIMISM

America is more wild and absurd than ever.

—Edmund Burke (1769)

The United States is ... a warning rather than an example to the world.

—Maria Child (1857)

The silent colossal National Lie that is the support and confederate of all the tyrannies and shams and inequalities and unfairnesses that afflict the peoples—that is the one to throw bricks and sermons at.

—Mark Twain, *My First Lie, and How I Got Out of It* (1900)

American pessimism sounds like a contradiction in terms. Demagogues and motivational speakers have long prated about the coincidence that the word "American" ends in "I can." (Of course, so do Costa Rican, Mexican, African, etc.) Nevertheless, though it runs against the grain of our national myths, American pessimism exists (and ironically finds its supreme expression in America's most beloved storyteller, Mark Twain), and has its own peculiar features. This serves as a reminder that pessimism is not a generic abstract formula, but a specific cultural project with endless variants. Things are bad in different ways; and pessimism reflects this.

As a minoritarian heresy, American pessimism is built on denials of some of the country's most cherished beliefs: our notion of ourselves as a new chosen people, with our supposed sacred history as a "city set on a hill," the last best hope of Earth, etc. In the face of such mythical pieties American pessimism is consistently irreligious. It stresses the still-bleeding wounds of our history ("We have met the enemy, and he is us"): genocide of the American Indians, slavery, environmental havoc, the ravages of the American Empire. And these aren't some sort of ancient events. Indians are still the poorest of Americans with the shortest life expectancy, blacks are in desperate shape, with sky-high rates of incarceration, unemployment, AIDS infection, and so on. Environmental degradation, under Republican presidents especially, has proceeded apace, despite the endless warnings of scientists. (People who direct their lives by theocratic myths, as Southern Baptists do, have a way of ignoring science. A majority of Americans still harbor serious doubts about evolution, but not about the Virgin birth.) And American armies are blasting the daylights out of Iraq.

In a significant moment at the end of his *Adventures* Huck Finn (before he was co-opted as the ultimate endearing All-American Boy) heads off on a doomed flight into Indian Territory—he's had enough of the cruelty and brutality of American "sivilization." As numerous episodes from the novel make clear, the "American Dream," whatever that exactly was, is over. Unfortunately for Huck, the frontier was just about to be officially closed.

America has been and still is a place of (potential) refuge for "the wretched refuse of your teaming shore," but only because of still more oppressive and chaotic conditions elsewhere, first in Europe, now mostly in Asia and Latin America. And Jews like Emma Lazarus, after being barred from the US in the 1920's and '30s, were left to perish in Nazi death camps. With its incalculable natural resources (left practically unspoiled till the 19th century) America has had enough unearned wealth to make its capitalists filthy rich and its middle class fairly luxurious, while exploiting the underclass and helpless minorities. In any case, a thinking person is obliged to maintain a certain a priori pessimism in the face of the ubiquitous optimistic lies about America. E.g., in presidential campaigns it appears that the American people are always by definition noble and wise; it's just that some of their shady politicians ("Washington insiders," captives of "special interests," and anybody not subject to term-limits) have unaccountably managed to ruin everything. But once the un-American rascals have been thrown out, like Jonah being heaved into the sea, all will be well.

This much-vaunted optimism is, it must be noted, not simply a matter of kitschy Hollywood happy endings and sentimental patriotism. There is an aesthetically respectable, however intellectually short-sighted, tradition of writers like Franklin, Emerson, Thoreau, and Whitman, etc., who have preached it in all sincerity. "Amerika, du hast es besser," Goethe famously proclaimed; and in many ways that once was true. *Some* American dreams (plural, lower case) came true; and many more deserved to, but didn't. American pessimism acknowledges this. It insists that if you fail to keep your promises—as this country blatantly has—you should, at the very least, apologize.

Mark Twain's ferocious anti-Christian barbs were, and are, an especially effective way of attacking American complacency, hypocrisy, and egotism, because so many Americans love to swathe themselves in Christian moralism and self-righteousness. The ultimate put-down of such mendaciousness is Huck Finn's hard-fought decision to defy his (societally poisoned) conscience and accept damnation by siding with a slave instead of his "owner," Miss Watson. Clear-sighted American pessimists will not be taken in by the hollow rhetoric of American religiosity, by such meaningless mantras as "God bless America"—what the Deity does with other, less privileged nation states is presumably His business (though if he treated all countries equally, we'd be in a fine predicament). God serves to validate our past crimes, our present policies, and our future plans. To which pessimism, says, "Not so fast."

American pessimists feel a particularly rueful taste in their mouth when they survey their country. If they belonged to an older, more jaded civilization, they could take its failures with more aplomb. (Up until Vietnam Americans liked to brag that their country had never lost a war—conveniently forgetting the dreadful Pyrrhic victory of the fratricidal Civil War.) Not anymore, with 2.1 million people imprisoned (an incarceration rate five times higher than Europe's), the military-industrial complex firmly in the saddle, the growing gap between rich and poor, the resurgence of evangelical fanaticism, the worthless and appalling kudzu jungle of popular culture—and all of this, apparently, serving to fuel our current strutting, narcissistic patriotism.

Such issues, however, are dealt with almost exclusively by the liberal press, where problems seem to be presented within benign rhetorical brackets, "We agree, this *is* the greatest country in the world—all the more reason for taking care of the blemishes." The only widely accepted mode for addressing the country's failures is the Christian language of sin and guilt. (Whence Lewis Mumford's suggested motto for the bicentennial celebrations of 1976, "Repent!"—which, while admirably non-self-congratulatory, assumes that redemption can still be had.)

This worked during the civil rights movement, but the most powerful Christian force in 21st century American politics is that of the flag-waving evangelicals, whose triumphalist vision of the USA as the New Canaan and themselves as the New Israel has reduced guilt to a private, moral (and mostly sexual) affair.

Looking for a quick illustration of why it makes sense to be a pessimist in present-day (2005) America, consider the morning "news" programs on TV. Monday to Friday one sees ebullient, placard-waving crowds cordoned off outside the Rockefeller Center studio of NBC's *Today* show, a mob of generally youngish, vociferous fans, smiling, cheering, and mugging for the camera—and thereby providing unshakable proof that the show is indeed *popular*. *Good Morning, America* used to round up beaming, well-scrubbed groups from across the country to pose together and bellow (of all things) "Good Morning, America!" As it happens, no talk show whatsoever can break for a commercial without its audience bursting into pointless scripted applause. (What exactly are they clapping for? The brilliance of the host? The charm or courage of the guests? The poignant new insights delivered since the last break?)

At any rate, the morning news ritual carries inanity to rare, though not harmless, heights. After the crowd's thunderous welcome has died away, we get a few minutes of perfunctory headlines, and then the usual absurdly protracted weather reports, both national and local. Ideally this tedious business will be jazzed up by some sort of "weather advisory," to guide clueless drivers on their perilous morning commute. The "news stories" that get covered next tend to focus on gossip (the legal vicissitudes of Scott Peterson, Michael Jackson, or Robert Blake), kidnappings or murders, rather than politics, on catastrophes (air crashes) if any are available, and easily graspable trivia (teen surfer attacked by shark), or heart-warming fillers (89-year-old great-grandmother graduates from college). Meanwhile, the real news, i.e., real trouble, the festering planetary problems of poverty, unemployment, child labor, AIDS, African genocide, nuclear proliferation and the rape of the environment, goes unreported. Pessimism, by contrast, wants to see things as they really are, even at the breakfast table.

But the real point of the morning news (apart from the musical entertainment or cooking demonstration in the last half-hour, by which time the serious members of the household have presumably left for work) is to teach the infantilized TV audience how to live. Without the endless medical advice and warnings, how would ordinary folk know how to shrink their waistlines, take care of their prostates, make it through menopause, evaluate hair-loss-replacement systems or chose the right gastroenterologist? After the medics (briskly interviewed by smart-ass anchor-people, whose questions show they already know most of the answers) have done their job, the morning news provides psychologists to straighten out your ailing love-life and raise your kids properly. Hollywood stars and best-selling authors try to seduce you into sampling their latest confection (how would you know what to watch or read otherwise?) Then come investment advisors, fashion gurus, travel consultants, computer geeks, and experts of every imaginable kind to guide the helpless lay person around the bogs and quicksands of modern life. The most powerful nation on earth seems to be populated by naïve imbeciles—for the pessimist that much is obvious.

Of course, everything that appears on commercial TV lives or dies by the Nielsen ratings. And absolutely every show, even if it doesn't grovel to the masses, has to have some seal of approval from them. We know that, whether visible or not, the crowd is always effectively there. With sit-coms we can hear it from the first instant on the laugh track (provided by an erstwhile "live audience"). This is an old story. Back in the early days of TV, Walter Winchell used to open his pseudo-news show by invoking a (non-existent) quasi-global audience: "Mr. and Mrs. North and South America," he would bark, "and all the ships at sea, let's go to press!" So, is perhaps the *Today* show just being honest (if more graphic) than others about its dependency on the viewers?

Naah. Just because the public has the last word wherever the majority rules, whether on market day or election day, doesn't mean it has to be so crudely and banally flattered. In Book VI of *The Republic* Plato makes the illuminating comparison of both politicians and sophists to an animal trainer. As Socrates says:

> I might compare them to a man who should study the tempers and desires of a mighty beast, which he feeds: he would learn how to approach and handle it, as well as at what times and from what causes it to get dangerous or the reverse, and by what sounds when another utters them, it is soothed or infuriated; and you may suppose further that when, by continually attending upon it, he has become perfect in all this, he calls his knowledge wisdom, and makes of it a system or art, which he proceeds to teach. (tr. Benjamin Jowett)

Was this a prophecy of public opinion polls, market research, and Karl-Rovean spinmeisters? Is there any alternative to it? Doesn't some portion of the public, at some level, find it sickening? Not in the USA, apparently. We're not taken aback by the sight of trainers constantly handing little munchies to their dogs or seals as they go through their routines. Atta boy! On the other hand, it might bother us to see the same sort of positive reinforcement being used on "nobler" creatures, such as lions, tigers, or elephants. Actually, there's something painful about seeing any wild animal—the domesticated ones have already sold out to humans—engaging in unnatural antics to amuse an audience and make a buck for the owners. (No wonder animal rights activists picket circuses. They're not just cruel, they're undignified.)

Which is roughly the impression left by the spectacle of the gleeful tourists on the *Today* show: they might as well be dancing bears (at least the bears don't try to be cute or pretend to be enjoying themselves). Don't they know they're being had? That they look ridiculous? And shame on NBC for continuing with such a boring, tasteless, predictable shtick to exploit them. Surely even quasi-journalists like Matt Lauer and Katie Couric would just as soon ditch the mob of supporters breathing down their necks? Now all we have to do is wait and see how long it takes before the trainer, the animals, or the folks at home get sufficiently embarrassed or disgusted by the act to put an end to it. Plato, and various American cynics, such as P.T. Barnum, H. L. Mencken, Sam Goldwyn ("Pictures are for entertainment, messages should be delivered by Western Union") and others would advise us not to hold our breath.

So, American pessimists are necessarily placed in a combative posture. They are, by definition, un-American, and therefore aliens in their own land. If nothing else, this gives them a still heavier burden of responsibility. In a country that—despite the above-mentioned 2,100,000 prisoners—has no prisons, only "correctional facilities," in a land where all children are "gifted" (in one way or another) and none are dull, much less "retarded," where *The American Heritage Dictionary* describes the term "deaf-mute" as "frequently offensive," where the adjective "fat" is banned from public school English readings, there's a special need for blunt truth-tellers, i.e., pessimists.

Finally, anyone in search of a Q.E.D. to validate American pessimism need look no further than the presidential election of 2004. What an astonishing combination of humbug, cant, and lies, hypocritical religiosity spoon-fed by a cynical, power-hungry clique to a passive, doltish multitude, and especially to that uniquely challenged group, "the undecideds," who fret and waver despite a mountain of evidence big enough to flatten Mount Rushmore (our supremely embarrassing national monument). And all this against the background of patriotic orgies, American flags in every lapel, speeches and spectacles glorifying the virtues of America, even as many countries around the world now view the USA, not unreasonably, as the ultimate threat to peace and stability. American pessimists might have to agree.

But, even if by some chance the American people were to belatedly stumble into wisdom (taught, perhaps, by some succession of unhappy events in George W. Bush's second term), it's not likely that they'll getting any closer to philosophical enlightenment. How many Americans, for example, could tell who said this: "Whoever has lived long enough to find out what life is, knows how deep a debt of gratitude we owe to Adam, the first great benefactor of our race. He brought death into the world"? It was, of course, Mark Twain, in *Pudd'nhead Wilson* (1894). Despite his Disneyfied image as a benign, adorably crusty patriarch, Twain was an outraged unbeliever, an anti-theist rather than an atheist, and a vehement denier of the after-life.

American pop-psychology would undoubtedly explain away his pessimism by recalling that he was emotionally broken by the string of deaths that ran through his life (his brother Henry, his infant son Langhorne, his grown daughters Suzy and Jean, and finally his adored wife Olivia). But for Twain death wasn't the problem, it was the solution. Like Solomon and Sophocles, Twain thought that the dead were the lucky ones, blessed escapees from the otherwise inescapable afflictions of life. Perhaps the most forceful declaration of his mortalist convictions comes in the sardonic *Letters from the Earth,* written in the last decade of his life but not published till 53 years later in 1963.

Here he attacks the cruelty of the Christian teaching on hell, which he sees as a sadistic disruption of the blissful unconsciousness of death. In the guise of Satan, Twain says:

> The first time the Deity came down to earth, he brought life and death; when he came down the second time [as Jesus], he brought hell.Life was not a valuable gift, but death was. Life was a fever-dream made up of joys embittered by sorrows, pleasure poisoned by pain; a dream that was a nightmare-confusion of spasmodic and fleeting delights, ecstasies, exultations, happinesses, interspersed with long-drawn miseries, griefs, perils, horrors, disappointments, defeats, humiliations, and despairs—the heaviest curse devisable by divine ingenuity; but death was sweet, death was gentle, death was kind; death healed the bruised spirit and the broken heart, and gave them rest and forgetfulness; death was man's best friend; when man could endure life no longer, death came and set him free.
>
> In time, the Deity perceived that death was a mistake; a mistake, in that it was insufficient; insufficient, for the reason that while it was an

admirable agent for the inflicting of misery upon the survivor, it allowed the dead person himself to escape from all further persecution in the blessed refuge of the grave. This was not satisfactory. A way must be contrived to pursue the dead beyond the tomb.

The Deity pondered this matter during four thousand years unsuccessfully, but as soon as he came down to earth and became a Christian his mind cleared and he knew what to do, He invented hell, and proclaimed it.

Reasonable persons could be forgiven for finding Twain's tormented fantasy a bit much, though its logic is impeccable: There is no notion of Hell in the Old Testament. If one accepts Christian orthodoxy, then Jesus is divine; and so "the Deity" can be said to be have invented and proclaimed hell on the strength of various passages in the Gospels (Luke 16.19-31, etc.) But if Twain (and the authors of not a few passages in Jeremiah, Job, Ecclesiastes, etc.) is right, and death is a blessed relief, then it seems fair to blame "the Deity" for cruelly depriving tormented mortals of surcease. Of course, the majority of Twain's mushy-minded optimistic fellow Americans who believe that heaven exists and they're going to swell its ranks, while preferring to soft-pedal the whole issue of eternal punishment, would no doubt find *Letters from the Earth* morbid, bizarre, and shocking. Their pessimistic brothers and sisters, however, already know how plausible Satan's (and Twain's) case is. Naturally, they also know that there's no hell or heaven outside the dizzy imagination of believers. By a pleasant, if not exactly novel, paradox, the pessimists wind up having a much saner and more positive view of life than *that*.

8

THE FILTHIEST NEST:
ECOLOGICAL PESSIMISM

Be fruitful and multiply, and replenish the earth, and subdue it:
and have dominion over the fish of the sea, and over the fowl of
the airs, and over every living thing that moveth upon the earth.

—Genesis 1. 28 (KJV)

The environmental impact of human beings depends absolutely
on just three factors: the size of the population, its per capita level
of activity, and the level of technology it employs. Biologist Paul
Ehrlich and physicist John Holdren of Stanford expressed this
rigid relationship as an equation:

Impact (I) = Population (P) x Activity (A) x Technology (T)...

According to every scientific measurement yet devised, the
biological health of the biosphere is currently in serious decline
due to the impact of human beings. The only way to reduce that
disastrous level of impact is to reduce the contributing factors in
the equation. And there lies the dilemma. We will not voluntarily
reduce our population, and we will not voluntarily reduce either
our individual level of activity or the level of technology we
employ, so that the I = P A T equation is, in effect, at its
minimum value right now. But by the year 2050 the global
human population, now almost 6 billion, will have grown by
20% to around 7.2 billion—at the very least. To maintain even
the present level of human impact on the planet under those
circumstances, the A x T component would have to be reduced
by a similar percentage (20%). But ... such a percentage is utterly
beyond us. Our primary energy consumption quadrupled in the

four decades between 1950 and 1990, and given the continued explosions of technology and consumerism, our accelerating energy demands show no signs of diminishing in the near future, in which case the next five decades will see us multiply our T factor by 2.5 at the very least. Therefore, with only the A factor remaining constant, we are left with the dismal prospect that by 2050 the impact equation—at its very best—will look like this: 1.2 P x A x 2.5T = 3 x I And if the present impact equals serious global damage, then three times the present impact surely equals global catastrophe. The tide of life has finally turned against us.

—Reg Morrison, *The Spirit in the Gene* (1999)

Anyone who's not an ecological pessimist by now must be deaf, dumb, and blind. Ever since we wandered out onto the savannahs of East Africa two million or so years ago, there's no doubt that humans have been, as Reg Morrison handily documents in *The Spirit in the Gene*, rehearsing for our current role as the ultimate plague species. Our hypertrophied brains will likely end by bringing about our own destruction; but until then, in the zero-sum game of who gets what space to inhabit, we've grabbed most of the room and thereby displaced our older and mentally slower siblings, the animals. And humans are the ultimate high-maintenance children of Mother Earth (though some are notoriously more so than others—Morrison's figures have one American consuming the same amount of natural resources as 120 Bangladeshis: all those SUVs towing all those powerboats to the summerhouse on Lake Humongous).

We live in a world of dwindling wildlife but countless pets and zoos, of billions of domestic animals raised to be slaughtered, eaten and otherwise processed into things we supposedly need; and there's no sign of a let-up in this pattern. Look at China and India (which would like to have as many cars and consume as much fossil fuel and animal protein as the US, though that would undoubtedly cause the planet to implode). Rapacious human monoculture proceeds apace.

The so-called Lynn White thesis blames our ecological woes on monotheism, specifically on Genesis' injunction to "be fruitful and multiply, and fill the earth and subdue it; and have dominion over the fish of the sea and over the birds of the air, and over every creeping thing that creeps upon the earth" (Gen. 1.28). Whatever the value of this argument (godless Marxists have done at least as much damage to the earth as true believers), it's correct in tracing the problem back to the arrival of humans on the scene.

But the human author of this text couldn't have dreamed how far things would go, although he did use the Hebrew verb root *kvsh*, which means "trample on," for what the English version softens to "subdue." As Schopenhauer emphatically put it in *Parerga and Paralipomena* 177: "Human beings are the devils of the earth, and animals are the tortured souls. This is the result of that installation scene in the Garden of Paradise."

But there's no need to single out the Bible on this one. Whether or not God, if he exists, ever ordered humans to behave as the owners and operators of the world, they have persistently, enthusiastically, ruthlessly done so; and never more than now. "Increase and multiply" seems to have been everyone's favorite divine command. Never mind that deforestation, desertification, salinization, strip-mining, destruction of animal habitat, pollution of land, water and air, overpopulation, global warming, gross waste and over-consumption, etc. ultimately ruin *our* "quality of life" and may very well lead to our extinction (the sooner, the better, truly radical ecologists might say—and all other species would surely agree). However many people make this indisputable connection and however much they try to stop it, their efforts are almost always overridden by the inert, powerless majority caught up in the struggle to make ends meet and, more to the point, by many individuals out to siphon off some short-term gain from the despoliation of nature. That group comprises not just banks, oil and mining companies, agribusiness, real-estate "developers," and such, but politicians and labor unions who see their millions of constituents' and members' needs as paramount.

In a secular world there are few words more sacred than "jobs" (until one recalls that building the ovens for Auschwitz provided jobs, as does the manufacture of billions of land-mines and all the other instruments of death). When Paradise gets paved, as it continually does, to put in a parking lot, asphalt-suppliers along with crane, bulldozer and steamroller operators post a nice profit. This is a familiar, boring truth, but it bears repeating because the environmental movement has long since won a kind of hollow public relations victory: Everyone is now theoretically in favor of "greening" (just as everyone is in favor of racial equality), but not of paying the price for it. People don't want nuclear waste in their backyards, but if they can make a pile selling those backyards to the builders of the next mega-mall, why not? You only live once.

In any case, all politicians have to do is nod in the direction of environmentalism, and then ride roughshod over the planet. Thus, the Bush administration, for example, labeled manifestly destructive programs "Clear Skies" and "Healthy Forests" Initiatives; and the protests, for the most part, went away. Bush appointed axe-wielding ecophobes to the soothingly-named Environmental Protection Administration; but the name on the door remained the same. And so on. Everybody loves the environment, although some, like Dick Cheney, think such love belongs in the realm of private virtue, as opposed to public policy.

We can see where this is leading and has, in many cases, already led: the poisoning of Minimata Bay and Love Canal, the drowning of the Hetch Hetchy valley in Yosemite National Park, the sucking dry of the Aral Sea and the effluent-dumping into Lake Baikal, the plight of the gorilla, the Indian lion, the California condor, the whales, sea turtles, Third World rain forests, coral reefs, glaciers, native grasses, and so on. Alfred Schweitzer seems to have been prescient when he wrote: "Man has lost the capacity to foresee and forestall. He will end by destroying the earth." Oh well, as long as we're not around to witness it.

Perhaps the best that pessimism can do here is slow down the pace of destruction a bit, make us aware of just how precious a treasure we are destroying, and heighten our enjoyment of it while it lasts. That would be something.

But the grounds for pessimism are the same as usual: given the basic dynamism of human life (to get and beget, finders keepers, losers weepers, looking out for #1, etc.), there's a heavy probability that the human race will ultimately come to grief—99% of all that species that have ever existed have already gone under. The curve of extrapolation stands right before our eyes; and most of us are hastening it on its way. The record of the past is bad, the present is worsening; so why in heaven's name, so to speak, expect a radical turnaround?

In any case, whatever the future brings, we now stand, and we and our children will stand, during our brief passage here, amidst the manmade ruins of a beautiful world. The only argument to be made against this devastating realization is the usual critique of pessimism: that it's demoralizing, that ignorance is bliss, etc. If we really think the planet is "cooked" (and all the evidence suggests that it's at least simmering), why bother trying to save it? Well, "saving" is out of the question, but even convinced pessimists will go on doing their bit to help the environment, just as most of them will go on, however illogically, having children and voting: instinct, the desire for short-term satisfaction, quixotic idealism, pigheadedness, you name it.

But there's no fooling ourselves. Just get in your car (any one of them) and drive out, preferably at rush hour, to some major local Desirable Destination. As you plod along, look at all the other drivers doing their best to overheat the planet, reflect on all the living soil that has been crushed and buried under the fat asphalt ribbon of highways, observe all the humanized, i.e., transformed-vanquished-eliminated nature around you, all the dwellings, emporia, offices, parking lots, and sterile storage huts, smell the exhaust-filled air, listen to the dull cacophony of the road, taste the perfect inanity, anonymity, and motoristic tedium of the moment, and say to yourself: "We've made it!"

Alternately, one could stay home and open the Bible, to Genesis, of course. "You will be like God," the serpent tempted Eve, "knowing good and evil." It seemed like a good idea at the time. After all, what sort of adult life can you lead if you can't tell good from evil? Were humans supposed to act forever out of blind obedience or brute instinct? Any self-respecting person would have eaten that fruit. Scripture itself (Psalm 8.5) says, "Thou (the Lord) hast made him (man) little less than a God." Anyway, they tried it and, as promised, "The eyes of both were opened." The problem is, the serpent was feeding Adam and Eve a fatal half-truth: they (we) *did* get to know good and evil, which *did* make them (us) like God, in a way; but it turned out that they (we) couldn't handle divinity.

The proof of this is the bloody mess we have made of the world. Take the Exxon Valdez oil spill (way back in 1989). We can't seem to prevent such disasters—we don't have the luck or the knowledge or the political will. We don't know how to manage the clean-up (Exxon still hopes that the tides and the wind and the rain and evaporation will eventually do the trick), assess the damage, predict the consequences, or punish the culprits. The media jumped all over Captain Joseph Hazelwood, who was drinking on the job, but he was only one link in a long and vulnerable chain of command.

These things happen all the time, no matter who's at the helm. Toxic wastes seep into our water, carcinogens invade our food, while the EPA monitors away. The First and erstwhile Second World ravage the land with smokestacks and bulldozers, the Third World does it with hungry livestock and collectors of firewood. Often enough the rich and poor, exploiters and exploited, *combine* pseudo-expertise and real poverty to wreak havoc, as in the building of the Aswan Dam, the ravages caused by the catastrophic incompetence of PEMEX or the clear-cutting of the Philippines.

In the process spectacular foul-ups like Minimata Bay or Bhopal or Chernobyl occur with relentless regularity. Murphy's Law isn't a joke; it's an axiom, a tautology in fact: sooner or later everything that can go wrong will go wrong. PCBs will wind up in cattle feed—and milk. Gun turrets and manned rockets will explode. Nervous radar scanners will mistake airbuses for fighter planes. And bland assurances from the technocrats that, except

for haphazard, irresponsible, totally avoidable "human error," we have
things under control are false.

We don't. Actually, we're like the sorcerer's apprentice: we've learned
some of the master's spells; how to get the magic started, but not how to
turn it off. (And who believes that the Sorcerer himself will arrive in time
to bail us out?) We can produce plutonium, but we can't get rid of it. We
can flood, but not drain, Glen Canyon. We can manufacture a thousand
mood-altering chemicals, but we can't persuade people not to take them.
We can manipulate our reproductive systems every which way, but we can't
stop crowding the world with too many babies. And so on.

Not the least ironic feature of all this is that our animal inferiors
—whom Genesis 1:28 bids us dominate—don't have such problems. They
do what comes naturally, and usually make out pretty well; or at least they
did until we came along. We've got the big brains, and we cause the big
trouble.

Animals (and primitive peoples, the few that are left) live on a "cash
basis" with nature: any major miscalculations and down they go. Only
civilized humans can accumulate the enormous, horrendous debts that we
can now have, recklessly spending in a decade the natural wealth if took
eons to make, greedily borrowing from posterity their fuel, shelter, and
sustenance. If God were to audit our accounts right now, he'd have to put
us into receivership.

But he won't. Ever since that bargain with the devil, like it or not, we're
in charge. We'd love to go back to Eden—imagine it: naked, carefree,
unashamed—but we can't surrender the knowledge that got us expelled in
the first place. We can't reach godhead, but neither can we shake off our
peculiar quasi-divine status. The best we can do is be more cautious and
self-critical (i.e., pessimistic). So here we are playing God with the earth,
while an audience of lesser creatures, seals, gulls, salmon, polar bears, et al.
scratch their heads in bewilderment: "Do these jokers know what they're
doing?"

Philosophers agree with Giambiattista Vico (d. 1744) that you can
understand only what you (or your congeners) have made; so we will never
fully understand either ourselves or anything else in nature. It's that simple:
we weren't in at the creation, and we can only guess what the formula was.
Once again the Bible (Psalm 139. 13) points the way: "I am fearfully and
wonderfully made"—and so is everything that exists, from gnats to nebulae.
We can't know the world as God does (if he exists), so we mustn't treat it
as if we did. Those filthy black Alaskan beaches, those limp sea otter
corpses, the whole nightmarish scene in Prince William Sound, framed by

the magnificent snow-covered Chugach Mountains, is a reminder—how many more do we need?—of what lousy gods we humans make. Pessimism is, among other things, a continuous call for modesty.

Postscript: On December 8, 2004 some 355,000 gallons of fuel oil were spilled off Unalaska Island into the Bering Sea.

9

ON AND ON AND ON:
PESSIMISM AND THE CONTINUUM

Our usual sloppy kind of observation takes a group of phenomena as a unit and dubs it a fact: between it and another fact it thinks up and adds on an empty space; it *isolates* every fact. But in truth all our acting and knowing is no series of facts with empty intervening space, but a constant flow. Now, belief in freedom of the will is quite incompatible with the notion of a continuous, unique, undivided, indivisible flow: it presupposes that *every individual action is isolated and undividable*; it is an *atomistic approach* to the realm of willing and knowing. ... Belief in freedom of the will—that is to say in *identical* and *isolated* facts—finds in language its constant evangelist and advocate.

—Nietzsche, *The Wanderer and His Shadow*, 11

Perhaps the truest words ever uttered by any human being are Heraclitus' (fl. ca. 500 B.C.) "All things flow." As Plato notes in the *Cratylus*: "Heraclitus says somewhere that all things keep moving, and nothing stands still; and, likening the things that exist to a flowing stream, he says you can't step into the same river twice." In the *Physics* Aristotle adds that, "And some say that it's not that some things move and others don't, but that all things are moving all the time, but this escapes our notice." In "The Mark on the Wall" (1921) Virginia Woolf graphically translates Heraclitus into modern terms: "If one wants to compare life to anything, one must liken it to being blown through the Tube at fifty miles an hour—landing at the other end without a single hairpin in one's hair! Shot out at the feet of God entirely naked! Tumbling head over heels in the asphodel meadows like brown paper parcels pitched down a shoot in the post office!" This principle, apart from its massive scientific and cosmological implications, could also be seen as the basis of pessimism.

In a notable passage in *The Gay Science*, 112, Nietzsche writes: "We do business with all sorts of things that do not exist, with lines, surfaces, bodies, atoms, divisible time, divisible space ... Cause and effect: such a duality doubtless never occurs—in reality we are faced by a *contiuum* from which we isolate a couple of pieces." But then again, as Nietzsche might have hastened to add, there are no "pieces," no "things" in any naively concrete sense. At one time or other we've all played the game of "degrees of separation," which proves that, link by link, everyone "knows" everyone else. But everything is connected to everything else, or it couldn't exist.

First, some brief reflections on how true this is. We can deal with the world only through language; and we know how language necessarily distorts: by creating isolated subjects separate from their verbs and objects and vice versa; by speaking of rigidly distinguished verb tenses (=*tempora*); in separating time and space (and in breaking them down into all sorts of discrete units), individuals and species, in a trillion arbitrary "takes" on the whirling flow of experience. And then, having distorted what's out there for the sake of practically manipulating it, humans deify their linguistic creations into things like essences, permanent names, inspired Sacred Scripture, immutable "laws," absolutely true statements, and the like.

The connection between this and pessimism is that our minds and hearts have, literally, nothing to hold onto, least of all ourselves; and that it's hard to endure this (but the sooner we do, the better). That makes Heraclitus' nickname "the weeping philosopher" appropriate, as opposed to Democritus (late 6th-early 5th century B.C.), "the laughing philosopher" (part of the reason for his laughter may have been the fact that he thought the world was made of atoms (literally, things that can't be cut into smaller bits), a kind of ultimate foundation, an unchanging core.

Humans quite naturally love to break up the flow, by taking pictures, for example, whose "reality" seems unimpeachable until we see one that flatly contradicts our notion of what the subject is "supposed" to look like. Or we see a snapshot after a long stretch of time; and we feel shocked (or amused) at the evidence of the instability of all things. We are thrilled by resemblances that turn out to be seductive illusions: nothing is, strictly speaking, identical either to an earlier or later version of itself or to anything else. The camera *always* lies.

We invent all sorts of partly arbitrary-partly natural units such as families, tribes, neighborhoods, or nations to frame our chaotic experiences and relationships. We make maps, mental and otherwise, of the world around us; all of them necessarily distort in one way or another; and they have to be, or should be, continuously updated. (Maps always lie too.) But that's a drag, so we don't usually bother, as long as they serve the pragmatic function of sooner or later getting us to more or less where we want to go, the same as with the collection of verbal cues with which we negotiate human relations ("How's it goin'?" "Wuddya say?" "Huh?" and other similarly crude signals). Our brains are full of wild misapprehensions (ask voters why they chose Candidate X, ask parents about their children and vice versa), but few of these are fatal; and we survive misreading our neighbor's character as we would *not* survive mistaking a minefield for a field of flowers.

We play the synchronized game of social interactions with even more deadly seriousness than the technically meaningless games of athletic skill, most of which are totally dominated by "the clock." Time itself may be the most absorbing, elusive, and maniacal of human inventions. It won't slow down at the good parts or fast-forward through the bad parts; there's no resolution to it, whence the attractiveness and futility of all visions of the "end time." The Greeks found the notion of infinity (the *apeiron*) repellent; just as we couldn't stand a work of art (or any object at all) without boundaries or shape; so we invent them and exaggerate all the lines we see flowing in and away from that direction; but there's no such goal for the world, except for the entropic one of our own Götterdämmerung.

Still, the most concrete result of the continuousness of reality is the problems it raises for belief in free will. If everything is as intertwined as the strands in a tightly woven fabric, the myth of individual autonomy falls apart. What becomes of the isolated moral subject, the individual moral act, personal free choice, when we and everything we do are just so many tiny molecules of H_2O in the roaring stream of life?

The debate over free will is as old as philosophy itself, if not older; and will obviously never be resolved. Even if the will were free, that could never be proved; because then it would have to be free out of necessity, a patent contradiction. And even though (mostly, if not entirely) false, it's an unshakable illusion. In many ways Nietzsche's position seems a reasonable one: what we call free will is the visceral rush we get from controlling ourselves and exerting power within and without us, the way the driver who turns the ignition key in a high-performance car and roars from 0 to 60 in 5 seconds feels he's in charge, even though he had absolutely nothing to do with constructing the car or the laws of physics and chemistry that it obeys in order to operate.

In any case, it doesn't really matter whether one believes in free will or not. What is absolutely beyond dispute is that the great bulk of human activities are programmed by nature and nurture. Whether there remains some small sacrosanct portion of the brain or soul or whatever that can be called "free" in any meaningful sense is a secondary issue. (William James, in a desperate flight of fancy, said that humans had at least the freedom to entertain one thought rather than another.) The more we reflect on the overwhelming power of both our genes and our environment, the more we realize that we're not "in control." We have to maintain the fiction of legal responsibility, because it undergirds our life in society. But it remains nonetheless a fiction.

How does this play into pessimism? Well, it wouldn't, necessarily, if there were some higher force directing everything for our own welfare, if life were a gorgeous symphony, and we were the players happy to have to play the flawless score, following all the tempi, etc. indicated by an all-powerful Composer-Director. But since this manifestly isn't the way things work, the fact that we have so little say in either our lives or the world as a whole (even while we're racked by the impossible desire for autonomy) leads to pessimistic conclusions.

Given that humans have the incorrigible habit of viewing themselves as both autonomous and capable of transformation ("It's never too late to … whatever"), it might be worthwhile to make a little list, in no particular order and by no means complete, of things that we can change either not at all, or only with great difficulty:

1. the fact that we were born at all
2. where, when, and how we were born
3. our parents and millions of other ancestors
4. our race, color, ethnicity, nationality, etc.
5. the circumstances of our childhood and youth
6. our gender and sexual preferences
7. our body type, height and normal weight
8. facial features, hair, eye color, etc.
9. language(s) first spoken
10. religion, if any
11. I.Q. and early education
12. congenital talents and deficiencies
13. number and nature of our siblings
14. diet and early nutrition
15. accidental injuries

16. genetic pre-dispositions and resistances
17. our likes and dislikes

And that's just for starters. The list could obviously be extended to infinity. Thinking about all this won't stop people who are strong or bright or athletic or beautiful or dexterous from thinking that they're somehow the independent authors or canny creators of their own qualities, since in fact they usually do various things to preserve and promote them. People notoriously love or hate or even kill themselves because of items in their physical appearance about which they can do little or nothing. But, in general, it's safe to say that the more we learn about the way the body functions, for example about brain physiology, the less room there is for naïve assumptions about freedom, and the more we realize how elaborately determined our behavior and sensations are. (Survival would have been impossible otherwise. If our brains had to stop and consciously make all the biochemical "decisions" that our livers make every second, we'd be dead.)

Just how un-free humans (or "other people," the ones who, in J.P. Sartre's dictum in *No Exit* (1944), *are* hell and whose behavior, seen from the outside, so often seems mechanical and ludicrous) can perhaps be best illustrated by the many instances where they fail to act in their self-interest. It would have been logical for the oppressed workers in early 20th century Britain, France and Germany, Russia and Austro-Hungary to make common cause against their capitalist enemies; but, of course, they killed one another by the millions while the ruling-class tycoons hid safely in their board rooms and sold armaments to redden the battlegrounds of WWI still more. Women have often played into the hands of oppressive males, for example by active, if not enthusiastic, participation in the rituals of clitoridectomy. American black soldiers have fought and died heroically for a country that denied them the status of equal human beings. Countless millions of people drink and smoke themselves to death while fully cognizant of what they're doing to their bodies. (Back in the 1950s Americans would offer one another cigarettes—now too expensive to be given casually away—saying, "Have a cancer stick.")

Here, as so often, the last word has to go to the non-pessimist Friedrich Nietzsche, who summed up his thoughts on free will in *The Twilight of the Idols*:

No one *gives* a person his qualities: neither God nor society, nor his parents or ancestors, nor *himself* ... *No one* is responsible for existing or for being made this way or that, or for living under given circumstances and in a given environment. The fatality of his nature cannot be teased out from the fatality of everything that was and will be. He is *not* the result of a special intention, a will, a purpose ... *We* invented the concept of "purpose": in reality *there is no* purpose ... One is necessary, one is a piece of fate, one belongs to the whole, one *is* in the whole—there's nothing that could judge, measure, compare, or condemn our being, because that would mean judging, measuring, comparing, and condemning the whole ... *But nothing exists apart from the whole!* ("The Four Great Errors," 8).

Of course, this won't stop us, or anyone else, from "judging, measuring, comparing, and condemning," any more than realizing the mythical nature of free will would bring an end to opinion polls, traffic tickets, jail sentences, or moral outrage. People will wind up marrying the exact sort of person any social psychologist with a small supply of data could have predicted they'd marry—and think the whole thing was stunningly original. There are practical and theoretical advantages in such thinking, however many contradictions they involve. Most moderns seem to agree that education solves all problems—or could, if we'd only let it. But this implies that children, and people of all kinds, will do whatever they're trained to do; which raises questions about, if it doesn't entirely expunge, free will. Raising children shouldn't, we think, be too different from baking. Get good ingredients, follow the recipe, keep your eye on the oven, and everything will (maybe) turn out fine. In any case, no one expects to put in a loaf of rye bread and take out a quiche. And so on.

Pessimism's final message here is: you're free, that is, you're not free, but you feel free; so feel free to stop worrying about all the ways that you're not free. The end results will be pretty much the same as if the fatalists were right; so relax.

10

Don't Kid Yourself:
Pessimism and Death

We are finite creatures with limited potential for satisfaction. Like cats, we love enclosed spaces and terminal movements; nothing pleases as much as a good beginning, a little progress along the way, and a cozy conclusion. The open-ended is a wound in the ordered world. Everything we deal with—sneezes and suppers and sentences—comes in small units, and we view the unfinished as gapingly incomplete. The infinite leaves us hungering for closure and sadly forgetful that everything is more precious when in short supply.

Why then would someone seek the infinite and want everlasting life? Only because intelligence has not extended its dominion over the heart. That we never perish and upon dying face a better life is an understandable hope of hard-pressed animals. That "we" in some sense are "immortal" may even be a proper object of faith. But it is a mistake to count on personal survival of death; and a pernicious error to think we need it to redeem this life.

—John Lachs, "The Vague Hope of Immortality"

The perpetuity of death is, needless to say, one of the anchors of pessimism and one of the rocky shoals for optimists. Christians and Muslims are dogmatically obliged to deny that death ends individual consciousness, though one wonders whether educated believers who talk about eternal life are thoughtlessly pretending or have just tabled the issue in their minds. Orthodox Jews speak of the World To Come, but with rather less gusto than other theists. (Jews in general don't seem to take the afterlife seriously.)

Otherwise few people go out of their way to affirm the obvious (isn't it?) fact that death is forever, with perhaps the majority of westerners, including godless intellectuals, taking refuge in a let's-change-the-subject agnosticism, as if they found the whole business excruciatingly naive. Stoics, if that breed still exists, may urge us (and themselves) to "abstain and sustain," while a modern-day Epicurean might advise us not to think about death at all, because, in the words of Epicurus himself, so long as you're alive, death doesn't matter; and once you're dead, *you* don't matter. One of Epicurus' most distinguished disciples, Michel de Montaigne, insisted that to philosophize was to prepare for death (I, xx), although later in life he seems to have gotten less preoccupied with the whole business.

Well, take your pick. Still, it's hard to avoid the commonplace notion that what doesn't last is no big deal. Plato pointed this out in both the *Laws* (804) and the *Republic* (Book X, 608): "Why, I (Socrates) said, what was ever great in a short time? The whole period of three score years and ten is surely but a little thing, in comparison with eternity. Say rather 'nothing,' he (Glaucon) replied" (tr. Benjamin Jowett). Of course, we have no experience whatsoever of eternity, except by extrapolation; but we do know our own smallness. If one could follow through on this belief, then life would be something like an anonymous practical joke. "The play is finished," said the emperor Augustus. "Draw the curtain, the farce is over," said Rabelais, or maybe he didn't. So, some famous folks on their deathbed tell us, life is farcical and not worth all the bother. On the other hand, if you get fully caught up in it, as natural selection has "designed" us to do, then the joke is on you. Either way, pessimism wins the day.

There are some paradoxical facts here that, however familiar, bear repeating. Once evolution stumbled upon sexual reproduction, with all its advantages (for the species), death became inevitable. Life is much more *interesting*, to look at if not to live through, once you open up all the possibilities of combining genes and playing the game of natural selection. But then, once you're born, you have to die (through apoptosis, or programmed cell-death); once you've passed on your genes, you're not needed; and at a certain point death often becomes highly desirable, for the survivors and the species, if not the patient. So fretting, or agonizing, about death would seem to be a major waste of time.

And clearly it is, but that doesn't change much. Any creature that calmly accepted its own extinction (as Buddhists are said to do, at least after long training) would never pass the tests of natural selection. So, we're meant to put up a fierce fight trying to do what we ultimately can't: survive. All of life is a quest for pleasure (i.e., mostly a flight from pain); and all pleasure is a matter of repetition. *Bis repetita placent*, as Horace said in the *Art of Poetry*. We want to enjoy ourselves over and over again. And so we try desperately to do so. As David Hume points out, it would be strange if Nature had trained us to fight tooth and nail against something that's actually good for us. So we must have reason to fear death, if only because the death of others deprives us of their presence.

That might not be a problem so long as we're caught up in the struggle for existence. One imagines that people such as the Chukchi, who live in the incredibly hostile and demanding environment of the northeastern tip of the former Soviet Union, would have little leisure for mourning the brevity of life or its frozen harshness. They're too busy herding reindeer or melting snow or repairing their tents. Angst is one of the gifts of urban culture. "Here in the city," cries Gilgamesh, "man dies oppressed at heart. Man perishes with despair in his heart, I have looked over the wall and I see the bodies floating in the river, and that will be my lot also. Indeed I know it is so, for whoever is tallest among men cannot reach the heavens, and the greatest cannot encompass the earth" (tr. N. K. Sandars).

Meditation on death tends to feed pessimism. Apart from the pain that frequently accompanies it, death is, most of the time, highly unaesthetic. (Of course, as Swift showed in his account of the Struldbruggs, endless old age unrelieved by death would be still uglier. "At ninety they lose their teeth and hair; they have at that age no distinction of taste, but eat and drink whatever they can get, without relish or appetite. The diseases they were subject to still continue ... In talking they forget the common appellation of things, and the names of persons, even of those who are their nearest friends and relations.")

In contrast to the satisfying blast or flourish or hum or high note at the end of a song or symphony, death is more often than not muted, shapeless and repellent. Traditional hymns end with a booming "Amen!" but how many lives just dribble away, for example into incontinence, dementia, and sleep? *Finem lauda*, says the old Latin maxim. Judge not the play before the play be done.

But by that standard the drama of life is a wretched affair. As Sherwin Nuland writes in *How We Die* (1994), there are no last words in the ICU. (But are there really many meaningful last words *outside* the ICU?)

Death, Thomas Mann reminds us in *The Magic Mountain* (1924), is more a concern to the survivors than to the (often unconscious) dying person. So, regardless of how well our own demise eventually goes (Julia

Child dying in her sleep at 92), by the time we reach adulthood we've probably started having bad experiences with death and already formed an opinion of death and of ourselves as "beings-toward-death"; and if we're honest, that opinion is likely a pessimistic one. Practically speaking, modern people are philosophical materialists, which readily translates into pessimists.

Since death is a human experience, and in a sense one that we have created, we can also reshape it in various ways (palliative care, barbiturate overdose, physician-assisted suicide, refusing to eat, Do Not Resuscitate orders, etc.); but of course there are severe built-in limitations here. In any event, one of the healthiest things we can do with death is abandon what philosopher John Lachs calls our "vague hope of immortality," which cruelly tantalizes us, while obscuring and distorting the contours of the only life we have.

Pessimism gets rid of such idle reveries and the sloppy thinking and feeling that go along with them. Once again, it banks on the overwhelming probabilities: consciousness, however defined, is never found apart from a properly functioning brain; and the brain, like the rest of the body, deteriorates with age, sometimes catastrophically, then dissolves in death. No brain, no self. All the so-called spiritual and intellectual functions of human beings, which we imagine as exalting us over all lower forms of matter, and grounding our claims for godlike status, cannot exist apart from the flesh; and, as Isaiah (among others) tells us, all flesh is grass.

This raises no particular intellectual difficulties when we survey other animals (and theists don't bother to include animals or plants in the afterlife); nor would it with us, were it not for our self-awareness. The patchwork of theories and images used to talk about life after death are the merest will-o'-the- wisp. Everlasting Life? (a contradiction in terms). The Immortality of the Soul? (What's a soul? Who's ever seen anything both alive and immortal?) The Resurrection of the Body? (Where and how and when will that happen?) The Last Judgment? (Traffic court for 80 billion people?) The Beyond? (Beyond belief.) The Next World? (And the next after that and the next after that and …) The Kingdom of Heaven? (How is that different from Pie in the Sky?) Good grief.

Such mythic fantasies all arise out of our inability to imagine, and our need to imaginatively prevent, our definitive disappearance. There isn't a gram of evidence to back them up; so why not dismiss them once and for all? We often let junk accumulate in our physical or mental attics, but once it starts spilling out all over and taking up space that could be used for here-and-now realities, it's time to throw it out. That may create an occasional emotional drag; but drugs, alcohol, and other forms of distraction can help. And knowing where we stand is usually better than being clueless. (Why else do sports-casters, and those little oblong boxes at the top of the TV screen, keep reminding us of the score?)

One final pragmatic note: there's a lot of anecdotal and literary evidence suggesting that at the hour of death—the outermost limit of human experience—believers have a much rougher time of it than unbelievers. The Middle Ages may have been the high water mark of Christian faith, but medieval poetry is full of variations on the theme of *Timor mortis conturbat me*: death inspires terror, not confidence. Boccaccio's account of the havoc wreaked by the Black Plague in Florence (1348) contains no scenes of anyone receiving pious consolation from religion at this supreme moment of agony. Of course, if Jesus himself died in agony, abandonment ("My Father, my Father, why has thou forsaken me?") and desolation of soul, it would be fitting for Christians to do the same.

The fact seems to be that Christians (like Dr. Johnson) have a worse time of it than atheists (like David Hume), because in addition to the inevitable terrors about falling into the abyss of non-existence, they have to deal with the added fear of Judgment and condemnation. Theoretically, believers should face the moment of death with all the confidence of Socrates about to quaff the hemlock —and then some (since he entertained the possibility that death might be an endless, dreamless sleep). But, while fantasies of otherworldly bliss are all but impossible to realistically believe in (except perhaps for Islamist suicide-bombers), it's all too easy to conjure up a scene of dreadful punishment for past offences.

Atheists and agnostics can strive for the equanimity needed to accept, if not welcome, their extinction; but believers are torn in opposite direc-tions, as they suffer both the instinctual fear of annihilation and the acquired fear of their Maker. Once again, the message of pessimism is more encouraging than people think.

Finally, let me add a personal note. I live in an urban neighborhood in upstate New York, with many tall maple trees and a large population of gray squirrels inhabiting them. Given the busy traffic and their heedless way of darting into the street, many squirrels get run over. Over the years as I've driven past the squashed, bloody corpses of squirrels, I've had the predictable spontaneous reaction: a shudder. (I myself have had, to date, only one accident with a squirrel, if that's what it was: late one night in August, 1974 I heard a sickening crunch as I drove over some small creature on an Idaho highway. I didn't stop to check if the squirrel or woodchuck or whatever had gotten away, but I doubt it.) Without knowing why, I've found the image of crushed squirrels lingering in my mind. I've wondered, for example, whether the years of vehicular carnage hadn't helped to breed a smarter and more savvy type of squirrel. Well, there were no obvious signs that they had.

Looking at the lifeless squirrels (as a rule the police or civic-minded neighbors removed them pretty quickly; but sometimes no one did, and then the corpse would gradually get flattened into an indistinguishable patch of dark fur), I often thought of the lines from Ecclesiastes: "For the fate of the sons of men and the fate of beasts is the same; as one dies, so dies the other. They all have the same breath, and man has no advantage over the beasts; for all is vanity. All go to one place; all are from the dust, and all return to the dust again. Who knows whether the spirit of man goes upward and the spirit of the beast goes down to the earth?" (Eccl. 3.19-21).

Of course, the "Who knows?" was a rhetorical question, and one look at roadkill was enough to answer it. Who could possibly imagine that the squirrel's "spirit" (and what would that be, exactly?) had gone "upward" or anywhere at all? Dead is dead. (In *An Essay on Man* Alexander Pope gently ridicules the "poor Indian" for thinking his "faithful dog" will accompany" him to the Happy Hunting Ground; we, Pope's readers, are presumably beyond such childish fantasies.)

By the same token, looking at pictures of brutally slain humans (the piles of emaciated corpses, for instance, in the documentary film shot after the liberation of Bergen-Belsen in April, 1945), how could anyone imagine that their "spirits" had taken flight to some realm of peace and beatitude? *This* had been a human being; now it had stopped functioning; end of story. The sight of dead bodies seems to be nature's bluntest and most brutal message.

Or is it? It didn't bother Thoreau, as he tells us in *Walden*:

> There was a dead horse in the hollow by the path to my house, which compelled me sometimes" [how long, as Hamlet might have asked, does it take a corpse to fully decompose and stop stinking?] "to go out of my way, especially in the night when the air was heavy, but the assurance it gave me of the strong appetite and inviolable health of Nature was my compensation for this. I love to see that Nature is so rife with life that myriads can be afforded to be sacrificed and suffered to prey on one another; that tender organizations can be so serenely squashed out of existence like pulp—tadpoles which herons gobble up, and tortoises and toads run over in the road; and that sometimes it has rained flesh and blood! With the liability to accident, we must see how little account is to be made of it. The impression made on a wise man is that of universal

innocence. Poison is not poisonous after all, nor are any wounds fatal. Compassion is a very untenable ground.

These lines (from the exultant concluding section called "Spring") are understandable, coming from a young man who was both tough- *and* tender-minded; but otherwise, to me at least, they stand self-condemned: Thoreau was not a tortoise or a toad, nor had he ever been speared by a heron. He had never witnessed any scenes of mass human violence (elsewhere in *Walden* he mocked war fever by pretending that when strains of martial music wafted from the town to his bean-field, "I felt as if I could spit a Mexican with a good relish"); and so he was free to revel in nature's extravagant waste of life, seeing it as "universal innocence." Thoreau would assure us that despite the hecatombs Schenectady will never lack for squirrels (though tigers and gorillas and blue whales may be on the way out), even as the world will never lack for people (in fact death can't keep up with our runaway numbers).

But, given the grisly history of the 20th century (even though most of us know it only secondhand), we have long since lost our innocence, and nature's along with it. Compassion may not be "tenable ground"—by now we should be used to the messy way that natural selection is carried out—but observing that process up close tends to drive us onto it anyway. Many of us, for example, have a hard time when our pets die.

In any case the whole issue clouds over when we realize that our compassion is limited to humans and other animals that we find appealing. Most of us, even squeamish vegetarians like myself, have no problem with slaughtering insects, especially the ones that invade our homes, property, or personal space. Blake may have written,

> Little Fly
> Thy summer's play
> My thoughtless hand
> Has brush'd away.
>
> Am not I
> A Fly like thee?
> Or art not thou
> A man like me?

but such sensitivity is too much for us (except for Jains, perhaps). We swat ants, gnats, flies, moths, mosquitoes, etc. without a second thought. Serves them right.

So then, as Monimus the Cynic (whoever *he* was), quoted by Marcus Aurelius (II, 15) emphatically said, everything is the way you take it (*panth' hypólepsis*). The fiercely Christian Blaise Pascal agreed when (with a sad shake of his head) he declared that, "Imagination decides everything." We weep at human deaths, wince at squirrels' deaths, and wink at those of insects. All grief, like all politics, is local. Mourning the slaughter of the squirrels is an understandable quirk, but it won't hold up in the court of philosophical reason (it's special pleading).

In any case the lesson remains: we die, that is, everything dies, forever. All the dreams of Krishna, Socrates, and Jesus founder on the evidence of—among other things—those squashed squirrels: mere rodents, but our mortal brothers and sisters. If there's any advantage to having such knowledge, we owe them a debt of thanks—or at least I do.

The truth of mortalism (amazingly enough., this ever-so-basic term still has to be defined for most educated readers: the refusal to believe in life after death) sometimes manifest itself with a peculiar force from quirky, trivial-seeming perspectives, like a sudden minor illness or the sight of noseless statues in museums or classical ruins. Once again I ask the reader's pardon for descending into philosophical doggerel:

> To Gogol's *Nose*—that's *nos* in Russian—
> we turn to launch today's discussion:
> One day, it seems, a nose took off
> and left its owner, Kovalyóf;
> it led him on a frenzied chase
> before returning to his face.
> Let Freudians and fantasts scheme
> to explicate that crazy dream.
> Don't miss *this* sense: a simple key
> for thoughts of our mortality.

> The nose is no essential part,
> like brain or liver, lungs or heart.
> The nose is fragile, boneless, weak,
> so quick to chill, so prone to leak.
> (And yet it sits so boldly there,
> so face-defining when we stare.)
> If, God forbid, a pimple grows
> and splashes crimson on your nose,
> your visage will be, ach, a mess;
> so give your nose a brief caress,
> and ponder this: the nose is like

our face's vanguard. When we strike
out on life's campaign, as we all know,
Our noses are "the first to go."
They're bumped and scratched at every point,
they're snubbed and twisted out of joint.
And once we're dead a few short years,
the nose just simply disappears.
The skin and cartilage decay
and noseless skulls come out to play.

   It's not just people, statues tend—
all sculpture left outdoors—to end
up noseless (vandals or erosion,
pollutants, or a bomb's explosion).
The same occurs, *si rien ne l'empêche,*
to phalluses of stone or flesh.*
Such tender organs' fate is rude,
because they, more than most, protrude.

   In any case, the nose goes first,;
so, you could say, its doom is worst:
It adumbrates us altogether,
the body's prow, the soul's bellwether.
Behold our frailest frontal thrust
before all else consigned to dust.

   And hence it serves to point a moral
with which no thoughtful soul can quarrel:
though humbly mute, except to sneeze,
it says, "Memento mori, please."
And, even when it goes, "Achoo,"
might that not be a coarse "adieu":
farewell, as if anticipating
our final breath's absquatulating.

   Professor Nose now leaves the hall;
his lecture casts a certain pall,
and yet its truth must be confessed:
it's plain as the nose—you know the rest.

---

*   And so one thinks, from time to time of that old vulgar German rhyme:
Wie die Nase eines Mannes,so auch sein Johannes.

11

BLOOD SOAKED ROOTS: CULTURAL PESSIMISM

Suffering from the cultural past. - Anyone with a clear sense of the problem of culture will suffer from a feeling like that of a person who has inherited an unlawfully acquired fortune or of a prince who reigns thanks to the violence of his ancestors. He thinks sadly about his origins and is often filled with shame and irritation. The sum total of the energy, joy, and will to live that he devotes to his estate is often balanced by a deep weariness: he cannot forget his beginnings; he looks to the future with melancholy: he already knows that his descendants will suffer from the past just as he does.

—Nietzsche, *Human, All Too Human*, 249

The following lines were, so to speak, inspired by Nietzsche:

There used to be a bumper sticker
(just seeing it produced a snicker):
"You bet your dupa I'm Polish!"
(Why not Chinese? Sri Lankan? Trollish?)
The murky joys of tribal pride,
refuse, it seems, to be denied.
We're oh so proud to be ... whatever:
for, come what may, one mustn't sever
those precious roots, those ties that bind
the motley mass of humankind
to their beloved blood and soil,

or *Blut und Boden*, but don't spoil
the mood with Nazi-flavored words—
please say "manure," not "shit" or "turds."

Yet here's a point one just can't skirt:
all culture's really based on dirt.
It may be rich and fruitful tilth,
but watch out for the noxious filth.
For every flower culture breeds,
it sends up twice as many weeds.
We rhapsodize on culture's foison,
but what about its deadly poison?

For culture kills (remember Cain);*
its specialty is causing pain,
although it saves its choicest dangers
for women, children, gays and strangers.
The mirror is its favorite gem;
 its favorite words are "us" and "them."

We can't list culture's every crime:
too boring, and who has the time?
But here's a modest résumé
of all the countless different ways
that culture (men in power) tries
to cut all women down to size:
control their minds—if that fails, blame 'em,
control their bodies—or else maim 'em.
Of all the things men fetishize
the hymen surely takes first prize.
A bride who lacks one may get stoned:
without it who can tell who's owned
by whom? The guys won't have *that* scanted,
(who wants to have his genes supplanted?)

The East likes harems, hijab, purdah,
and, if that won't work, plain murder,
(Muhammad blesses battery).   Qur'an 4.34
You like high drama? Try suttee.
North Africans prefer to slash

---

* Gen. 4.10: "Cain ... built a city."

the clitoris: the sacred gash
to choke off climax with a bleed
(who knows where things like that might lead?)
Another method, found worldwide,
i.e., female infanticide,
has neatly trimmed the girl-excess—
one hundred million, more or less.
The West is less inventive here:
machismo, rape, and programmed fear,
the lure, the whip, the bribe, the fine,
are used to keep the gals in line.
(It takes a bit of bravery
to flee from privileged slavery.)
Genteel oppression is the norm:
by hook or crook make them conform.

    And so it goes. You might say, "Wait.
There's no need to exaggerate.
The sexist curse is fading fast;
the double standard just won't last.
Why sweat about a few mad mullahs?
Don't amazons trump ayatollahs,
(Iranian and otherwise,
those boring, bearded, scowling guys)?"

    Don't be too sure; in any case
bad culture-karma spreads apace.
It's still as toxic as before,
we're still infected to the core.
We're drunk on culture, boozed on bias,
which always sounds so sweetly pious:
those books and hymns, those catchy rhymes
(what's culture got to do with crimes?)
We pass it on, as our life fades,
like stocks or bonds or jewels—or AIDS.
You think we'll soon escape this stupor?
Could be, but still: don't bet your dupa.

    Like Nietzsche's prince, we stare aghast
back into culture's bloody past,
and forward, full of melancholy,
to future times of vicious folly.
We moderns relish our "estate,"
although it comes with such grim freight:

injustice, terror, grief, and loss
(from Hammer-Sickle, Crescent, Cross,
and other symbols of *la Gloire*
from culture's lethal repertoire).

How many of the world's "great men"
were really less than human, then?
Admire Cheops' pyramid:
one doubts the slaves who built it did.
Napoleons and Hannibals
were just colossal cannibals.
"Marse Robert" wins the South's applause:
that butcher for a stupid cause.
We sing, "Land where our fathers died"—
a land they got through genocide.

So our descendants—those with brains
and hearts—are doomed to feel the pains
of culture's poisoned gifts: the ones
that keep on giving ... countless tons
of bitter karma. Or, still worse,
think of the past and its great curse
as felt, not by some moneyed toff,
but some poor wretch with no days off:
the prince has lots of golden buffers,
the prole turns to the wall and suffers.
S/he bears the burden of the past,
crushed then, crushed now, crushed to the last.

In *Civilization and its Discontents* (1929) Freud argued that living under the innumerable constraints of civilized life (or *Kultur*) gave rise to all sorts of malaise (*Unbehagen*), which rational adults had to put up with, as the painful price of peace and order. As he watched the rising tide of violent anti-Semitism in Vienna between the Wars, Freud became understandably alarmed; and he may be forgiven for assuming that the problem was simply one of getting the proto-Nazi gentile hordes to conform to time-worn standards of decent behavior. But Freud, who fortunately died of a doctor-provided morphine overdose for his incurable cancer of the jaw in 1939, before the outbreak of World War II and the Holocaust, never seems to have surmised that culture itself, *all* cultures, might have been at fault, not just restive individuals and mob-like groups.

Pessimism is more than ready for that surmise, and it has no qualms about skewering the sacred cow of "culture." "Cultural pessimism" could mean any number of things; I use it here to mean an intense skepticism, as forceful as, but more nuanced than, the famous Nazi quip, "Als ich 'Kultur' höre, entsichere ich meinen Browning" ("Whenever I hear the word 'culture,' I reach for my pistol" or, more precisely, I "release the safety-catch on my Browning"). This is especially needed nowadays because "culture" has become such a soft and fluffy term. It can refer to almost any entity, a company, for instance, a TV network, or a school. And it's often appealed to sentimentally by minorities in search of their "roots." The tender-minded champions of culture (and multiculturalism—the more cultures, the better!) don't seem to have noticed that all cultures are by definition self-centered, deeply biased in countless ways, and responsible for much of the world's ongoing misery.

A good example of this would be the virulent machismo of sub-Saharan African cultures, which has played so large a part in the spread of AIDS and the suffering of women, and which has done more than a little damage in Afro-American life. By an understandable twist of fate, mistreatment by strangers seduces people into inventing air-brushed idealizations of their past. Disgusted by the legacy of slavery, blacks shed their white slavehold-ers' names and borrow Arabic names, oblivious of the huge role played by Muslim traders in the enslavement of some 16,000,000 Africans (with more than a little help from black middlemen). But then American WASPs also boast about their slave-owning Founding Fathers. Amerindian cultures have been canonized and elevated beyond the reach of criticism (torture of prisoners? gross sexism? naïve ethnocentricity?) Contemporary Japanese believe *they* were the victims, not the aggressors, in World War II, and so on.

By a dubious logical leap, culture gets cut loose from history, as if it were some sort of gorgeous museum, a timeless aesthetic treasure-trove, apart from all the things members of that culture have done in its name and under its inspiration. "Culture" becomes trivialized into a series of rituals, literature and art-works (as if all *those* things were morally neutral), into colorful, picturesque behaviors: tribal dances (generally all-male affairs), hunts (e.g., the Washington State Makah Nation's grotesque slaughter of gray whales with bazookas in 1998), traditional mutilations, bloody sacrifices (to non-existent gods), and so forth, regardless of the damage they do.

As with history, it's impossible to quantify the net positive and negative impact of human cultures, insofar as we have records of them. It would, however, be fair to note that the most primordial form of culture—agriculture—has proved, in the long run, an unmitigated disaster for planet earth. Animal husbandry (substituting eight pounds of grain for one pound of fatty beef, feeding pool-raised salmon five pounds of wild fish to get one pound of second-rate "cultivated" fish, etc.) has been the worst offender in this regard; but draining wetlands for cropland, slash-and-burn devastation of the rain forests, manmade Dustbowls with blown away topsoil, overuse of fertilizers, squandering aquifers for irrigation, dam-building, and so forth, have all gravely wounded the environment. (Thus far the world's farmers are unrepentant.)

So, of course, have the frenzied consumerists of First World societies, with their absurd proliferation of pavement, roads, cars, clothes, houses, boats, and toys of every sort. Satisfying the insatiable appetites of rich consumers apparently requires the enslavement of Third World workers and the despoliation of their landscapes. Rich countries can afford to have national parks and zoos, poorer countries can't, except as part of the tourist trade. So it seems safe to predict that eventually there will be no large predators roaming the wild, i.e., there will no longer *be* a wild in the proper sense.

Beyond the damage they inflict on the world around them, human cultures also hurt and mangle humans, through customs like slavery, female infanticide, clitoridectomy, "honor" killings, child marriage, polygyny, tribal violence, capital punishment (and the penal system in general), legalized oppression of workers, regressive tax codes, and so on. As mentioned, in *Civilization and Its Discontents* Freud argued that the key task of culture is to tame the human beast and create order out of the swarming societal mass of conflicting ids. Humans don't like giving up (or even deflecting or sublimating) their deeply programmed desires; so to the extent that we become civilized, we are bound to get frustrated and cranky. Too bad, thought Freud.

Would that things were so simple. There are two huge problems here: Culture could be seen as simultaneously too lax and too harsh, too lax because it fails to keep us in line, to maintain minimal standards, too harsh, because much of what has long been, and still is being, done in the name of "socialization" things like establishing rigid, warped gender roles, beating children, religious indoctrination—is plainly sick. Too harsh again, because, granted that various kinds of repression-and-suppression, from weaning to toilet-training to teaching morals and manners, are necessary to make life livable, don't all our lives contain far too much of what Herbert Marcuse calls "surplus repression"?

If the whole point of life is to create an efficient libidinal economics, to maximize pleasure and minimize distress, then modern workaholic bourgeois culture isn't doing a good job. In both cases society is mistreating its members with good intentions, in the name of some ideal or god or sacred tradition. But nowadays it's a rare generation that doesn't think its parents did some fundamentally wrong things in their *paideia* (the Greek word for education, which can also mean "correction" or "chastisement," i.e., beating, which was the stock in trade of all ancient educators); and any of us could rattle off a long list of mistakes that older, less enlightened generations habitually made.

This is the cultural basis for pessimism: the sober realization of how much has gone wrong, the cold-eyed recognition of how little we can do about it, the refusal to entertain inflated, unrealistic expectations of a brighter tomorrow, the calm determination to make the most of a bad bargain.

12

DON'T BE DUPED:
PESSIMISM AND COMEDY

> This world if a comedy to those that think;
> a tragedy to those that feel.
>
> —Horace Walpole (1776)

Pessimism would seem to be gloomy by definition, a sort of incessant philosophical groan; but it needn't be that way. An ancient western (and biblical) tradition that runs from before Aristotle to beyond Henri Bergson sees the essence of comedy as the jolt of pleasurable superiority (Thomas Hobbes's "sudden glory") we get from observing the fools all around us. (The Old Testament likes to mock the stupid idol-worshiping goyim.) In that sense comic pessimism would be intellectual amusement at the absurdities of human life (with a big dollop of scorn for the infantile optimists who just don't get it).

Humans are notoriously uneasy blends of ape and angel. The classic image for this would be something like a pope, the sanctimonious, ethereal Pius XII, say, suddenly attacked by diarrhea or displaying a prominent hard-on at a pontifical mass. The theme runs all the way through western literature (one of Rabelais' oaths invokes "the Virgin [Mary] who hoists her skirts"). Among the countless evocations of this impossible dichotomy is the string of sublime commonplaces supplied by Alexander Pope in *An Essay on Man*, Book II, 2-18:

> Placed on an isthmus of a middle state,
> A being darkly wise, and rudely great:

With too much knowledge for the skeptic side,
With too much weakness for the Stoic's pride,
He hangs between, in doubt to act or rest,
In doubt to deem himself a god, or beast;
In doubt his mind or body to prefer,
Born but to die, and reasoning but to err;
Alike in ignorance, his reason such,
Whether he thinks too little, or too much;
Chaos of thought and passion, all confused;
Still by himself abused, or disabused;
Created half to rise; and half to fall;
Great lord of all things, yet a prey to all;
Sole judge of truth, in endless error hurled;
The glory, jest, and riddle of the world!

Of course, like one of his sources, Pascal ("What a chimera human beings are!" etc., *Pensées*, 434), Pope takes much of the bite out of this notion by presuming the existence of an omniscient, omnipotent God to resolve such contradictions and provide a (potentially) happy ending. But if one sees this bundle of tensions and troubles as fundamentally irresolvable, then a comically pessimistic perspective ensues.

Self-consciousness is the ultimate joke. It inhibits our performance as animals (we're followed everywhere by our own team of gawking paparazzi). It strains for the unattainable ("More! More!" Blake wrote, "is the cry of a mistaken soul, Less than All cannot satisfy Man"). It has infinite reach, but hopelessly limited grasp. It makes us miserable with hope, guilt, envy, resentment, etc. It enables, and sometimes forces, us to live in the past and the future, which by definition don't exist. (But does the present exist either? St. Augustine famously chased after the ever-fleeting vanishing point of the present, which is gone as soon as one says, "Here it is!" So what's to hold onto?) Whatever advantages our brain may give us over the rest of the animal kingdom, its cost appears to be prohibitive. But nobody wants to give it back.

Deep within our proudest achievements lie elements of farce. Tests have repeatedly shown that communication (the key to our superiority over the beasts) is mostly miscommunication (that in itself is a major source of comedy), thanks to the ambiguity of verbal symbols, tone, facial expressions, gestures, etc. Our ideas are an absolute muddle. Our most sweeping and grand thoughts (religious beliefs) are palpably false (cf. Genesis 1-3). We feel godlike in our attempts to pierce the secrets of the universe, but keep seeing our own face peering anthropocentrically back at us, framed by space and time and all sorts of built-in human biases. Tender-minded observers might find this tragic, but pessimism grins and bears it.

One obvious instance of this would be the Theater of the Absurd, where human destiny is depicted as too miserable to qualify as comedy, and too ridiculous to be tragic, whence the tragicomedy of *Waiting for Godot* (1952) But there's a broad pessimistic, even nihilistic, streak in all comedy. Clowns, like Strepsiades in *The Clouds* or Rabelais' Panurge or Puck or the Good Soldier Šveyk or Harpo Marx, are not cute, non-threatening entertainers; they're anarchists through whom we vicariously indulge our bomb-throwing, destructive impulses from the safe hideout of an easy chair.

The traditional explanation of the violent-horseplay side of comedy is that it serves as psychic release: we can vent our anti-social feelings and then go back to work. (Aristophanes' wild utopian fantasies, such as *The Birds*, are clearly meant to be enjoyed but not to be taken out of the theater and cashed in as a down payment on obtainable goals.)

But in the modern west there's no returning to the ancient comic vision, which assumes that the world, for all its twists and turns and hard knocks, is basically "o.k." Cervantes, for example, grounds his sublime comedy in the assumption that, when all is said and done, we know the difference between the real and the imaginary, between the nightly news and novels, and that, much as we all enjoy temporary flights into the fantastic, only madmen can't tell the difference between the two. *And* that's not a problem. If lunatics like Don Quixote (who in his many lucid intervals is a highly intelligent and marvelously eloquent man) break a few bones, their own or others', when they plunge into their fantasies, so what? Putting it another way, Cervantes (and other great comic writers, like Rabelais and Shakespeare) was not about to second-guess the creator, something that moderns do all the time—that's in fact one of the hallmarks of modernity.

The Hebrew Bible invented the happy ending (the Messianic kingdom); and Christianity thumpingly reaffirmed it (cf. the Book of Revelation and *The Divine Comedy*). But, again, in modern discourse the term "happy ending" is often used contemptuously or at least dismissively; it suggests something contrived, sentimental, and unreal. Modern comedy, except for the cheap commercial kind, tends to be bleaker than the classical sort. And so it would be safe to call it pessimistic. Anything less than that would be and is, in fact, self-deception. Erich Segal undoubtedly went too far when he said (2001) that comedy is now dead, but a classical scholar could be forgiven for overstating his case like this. The grand life-affirming vision and power of classical comedy certainly *is* dead. (Among other things, who can believe in the idea of a benign and all-wise patriarchy divine, human, or both, presiding over our destiny, as so many classic comedies do?) Pessimists know this is too good to be true, and they laugh (in Hobbesian superiority) at the all the benighted folks who don't. Of course, in a broader sense the whole point of pessimism is that the joke is on us.

The perfect illustrator of this cosmic joke is Franz Kafka, who is forever putting his protagonists (all versions of himself) into ridiculous situations, which could all, it seems, be exploded or escaped if the lead character would just stop playing along with the system. In *An Imperial Message*, for instance, the dying emperor *seems* to want to send a final word to an unnamed recipient; but at the same time there's no credible way the messenger will ever make this way through the labyrinth of the Celestial City (if that's what it is). "Nobody can get through here," says the narrator in *An Imperial Message*, "especially not with a message from a dead man.—But you sit by your window and imagine it to yourself, when evening comes." Which prompts the following philosophical jingle:

> The brothers Tolstoy had a game
> whose outcome always was the same:
> they'd crawl beneath a covered table
> and test how long they might be able
> to block all thoughts, while hunched down there,
> about a giant polar bear.
> Of course, a veto of this kind
> brought—instantly!—the bear to mind.
> Some bold ideas, however silly,
> grab our attention, willy-nilly.
> The only way that you can win
> this sort of game is ... don't buy in.

> But think how many other notions
> get charged with hopeless, wild emotion
> and likewise commandeer our head:
> "Can soul survive when body's dead ...?"
> "Perhaps we lived before our birth ... ?"
> "Is there a Heaven linked to earth ... ?"
> or "Could God send—he must have ways—
> infallible communiqués?"
> "Suppose there were a loving Savior,
> *might* He *reward our good behavior ... ?*
> *How splendid all those visions seem.*
> *Alas, they're just an idle dream—*
> *like, f'r instance, finding polar bears*

ensconced in *our* dens, not in theirs.

The flaw in all such speculation
is that it's born of desperation:
attempts, all doomed, to pierce the veil
of maya, vault across the pale
of human language, human things.
(Can pigs ascend on eagles' wings?)
If one could trust to human hopes,
then words would serve as telescopes
to pierce the depths of outer space;
but they're just mirrors, and the face
that grins at us is ... ours. Too bad:
we want what no one ever had.
Cervantes calls this *pan trastrigo*—
a bread that can't be baked, *amigo.*

Franz Kafka tells a story a-
bout this very same aporia:
a dying emperor (the Lord?)
has one last favor to accord
to you—a message from on high;
and so he calls his envoy nigh
and whispers it into his ear;
the man's about to leave, but here's
the hitch: he's blocked, he barely moves,
he seems to spin through endless grooves.
So will he ever get to you
—and is the story even true?

Most likely not, but nonetheless
you wait and hope for his success.
That's your mistake—or Kafka's: he
just kept on hoping foolishly.
Well, no, in fact, he clearly twigged
he had no chance: the game was rigged.
But still he craved the herald's voice;
he felt he really had no choice.
Which leaves us right where we began:
when lured like this, you always can
refuse to play. Why bother, man?

You know, it's like eternity:
the Bible* says, the Deity
invented it to give us fits.
No doubt, still we can keep our wits
by holding firm to this arrêt:
we must remember to forget.

Since the stable, wisely ordered world of classical comedy has gone for good, we'd best let it go. To be sure, there's more to comedy than superiority. One can laugh out of pure pleasure, as a baby playing peekaboo does, out of relief (HIV negative!) or exultation (Sox Win Series!) or relatively unselfish delight (Good for you!) Pessimism has no objection to any of that—if you can get it. But having your leg pulled—repeatedly—by God, the universe, destiny, or whatever is no fun at all; and pessimism provides an antidote for such a bitter situation: if not exactly the last laugh, at least the ability to say, "Oh, I've heard *that* one a million times before."

---

* Ecclesiastes 3.11. "He (God) has made everything beautiful; in its time; also he has put eternity into man's mind, yet so that he cannot find out what God has done from the beginning to the end."

13

THE TRIUMPH OF
EXPERIENCE OVER HOPE:
SEXUAL PESSIMISM

Youth is customarily called the happy time of life and old age the
sad time. That would be true if the passions made people happy.
But in fact they rip youth back and forth, with little joy and much
pain, … On the other hand it could be said that the after the
sexual drive has been extinguished the actual core of life has been
consumed and only the shell is left, so that it's like a comedy that
begins with human beings and is later played out to the end by
automata dressed in their clothes.

—Schopenhauer, *Aphorismen zur Lebensweisheit*, Ch. VII

How do you expect mankind to be happy in pairs when it is
miserable separately?

—Peter De Vries

Everything ever said or written about love and sex is a cliché. That
can't be helped. But there's truth in all clichés, and a pattern emerges
as we study them. One might as well begin with *A Midsummer Night's
Dream.* Lysander's wimpy complaint, "The course of true love never did
run smooth"—may be a parody of a lover's lament (by the way, what
exactly is "true love"?), but it's a statistically credible statement. The odds
against long-term sexual fulfillment are, shall we say, high. In western

literatures comedies end with a wedding, or used to. Tragedies (Jason and Medea, Paolo and Francesca, *Madame Bovary, Long Day's Journey into Night, Lolita*) begin with one.

And why not? The myth of perfect love, of ecstatic sexual harmony, as seen in *l'amour courtois*, is essentially unattainable, except very briefly, and then only in the teeth of society's opposition (in a world of ecstatic lovers no work would ever get done); and such love must end in death. In fact, the lovers themselves seem to *want* to die: there's no way the flame of passion could burn on, year after year, through childbirth, menopause, and relentless physical and mental deterioration.

As always, humans aren't satisfied with their genetic program, the way animals are. They have to mythicize it (i.e., add *mythoi*, words and stories and fantasies) to it. That makes life interesting, but it also guarantees failure. Romantic love, for obvious reasons, was never in nature's plan. It's not needed for procreation; only male orgasm, or, still less, ejaculation of enough sperm with enough motility into the vagina at just the right time of the month. (If evolution had been more romantically inspired, it might have located the clitoris so that the female orgasm resulted directly from vaginal penetration.)

But romantic love, that sublime, narcissistic *folie à deux*, is a matter of psychology, not anatomy. It's not concerned with having, raising, and protecting offspring. It's not concerned with offspring at all. The Victorian notion of fusing romantic love with marriage was brilliant poetic conceit and a vast improvement over many older models of marriage, such as the traditional ownership of women by men or the Pauline notion that "it is better to marry than to burn [with lust]" (1 Cor. 7.9) with its absurd idealization of celibacy and virginity.

But we can see through all this. Flight from world into a "love-death" *is* a way out, but a problematic one. Most forms of romantic love still enslaved women. J.S. Mill's cool but devastating analysis of women's connection to man, written almost a century and a half ago, has lost none of its bite:

> When we put together three things—first, the natural attraction between opposite sexes; secondly, the wife's entire dependence on the husband, every privilege she has being either his gift, or depending entirely on his will; and lastly, that the principal object of human pursuit, consideration, and all objects of human ambition can in general be sought or obtained by her only through him, it would be a miracle if the object of being attractive to men had not become the polar star of feminine education and formation

of character. And, this great means of influence over the minds of women having been acquired, an instinct of selfishness made men avail themselves of it to the utmost as a means of holding women in subjection, by representing to them meekness, submissiveness, and resignation of all individual will into the hands of a man, as an essential part of sexual attractiveness. (*The Subjection of Women*, 1875)

Given this unequal distribution of power, which is still in effect practically everywhere, it's no wonder that male-female relations should be so troubled, not to say poisoned. Heterosexual unions and family life have been a school of slavery for women. And this isn't going to change any time soon for a majority of women on the planet, especially with the resurgence of Islamic (and Judeo-Christian) fundamentalism.

But even granted the slow spread of something approaching equality between the sexes, the problems remain daunting. Some couples say they've found lasting felicity—and good for them, assuming they're telling the truth—but that wouldn't change the pessimistic probabilities. We might not want to go as far as the Rev. W.H. Brookfield, a mis-mated friend of Thomas and Jane Carlyle, who said that getting married was "dipping into pitcher of snakes for the chance of an eel." But many spouses would have to echo that jaundiced judgment; and while trying to beat the odds, pessimists would at least be aware of them.

Women especially can't fail to have noticed that the obsessive focus on sexual passion in the myth of courtly love conveniently masks their powerlessness everywhere outside the bedroom. It's as if the utter dominance of men in all political, economic, and social spheres eventually struck even males as boring, if only for story-telling purposes. So they fashioned a make-believe narrative realm where women were allowed to exert their (undeniably real) sexual power over men while ignoring, or pretending to ignore, their subordinate status. In the rhetoric of courtly love women were, and still occasionally are, addressed as "queen" and "empress." They are "worshiped" and "adored." Men fall on their knees before them, and so on. But there can be no marriage or childbirth in this domain because that would drag everyone back into patriarchal reality. Hence all romantic love has to be "forbidden" (which usually means adulterous, or at least hedged about by daunting obstacles). It never intersects with everyday occupations (whence the provocative T-shirt slogan, "Make me late for work"). And, by definition, it never lasts very long, because nobody could spend an entire life in a high fever; and our patience in watching erotic ecstasy is limited.

In recent years pornography has replaced romantic love as the central mythic playground for sexual love. Porn "liberates" women by turning them into ravenous nymphomaniacs who fling themselves at (usually far less attractive) men, whose slightest touch drives the women (slender-curvaceous, with shaven pubes, but often sprouting repellently bulbous breast implants) into a round of pseudo-orgasmic writhings and moans, culminating in the bliss of having their partner(s) squirt semen into their mouths or onto their upturned faces. The overall impression most porn creates is that it's attempting to squelch that old bugbear, feminine power. In the real world women still have the maddening ability to both arouse and refuse their male admirers. Rape is one solution to that problem, but most men feel, at least in theory, a bit sheepish about resorting to it. But, thanks to the now gigantic porn industry, men can finally get whatever they want, on videotape or DVD anyway, with no backtalk.

It's true that this comes at a certain price. Pornography dispenses with personal emotion, except the most transparently faked and cheesy sort. In fact, the key to the whole process seems to be impersonality: the creation of a disappointment-free zone where none of the usual bothersome features of human interaction (past wrongs endured and unforgiven, conflicting agendas, personal incompatibility, "performance" failures, and so on) ever intrude.

True, someday a non-grossly-sexist brand of pornography might be produced, a pleasant, harmless genre depicting and celebrating the remote possibility of a dazzling sexual utopia—ideal instructional tapes, as it were. On that playing field men and women could enjoy real equality (forgetting women's superior orgasmic capacity). Till then, pornography, or rather its fabulous popularity, simply shows, along with other data, like the divorce rate and the decline of traditional marriage, just how far men and women remain from getting their act together. (And there's no evidence to suggest gay persons are doing much better.) The lovers, the male ones anyhow, do protest too much. So the case for pessimism, here as elsewhere, remains strong. Pessimism rightly suspects all attempts to drag heaven down to earth. It urges people to question their own motives, distrust tradition, compromise as much as possible, and, alas, lower their expectations. If nothing else, that might lower the incidence of wife- and girlfriend-beating, "honor killings," murder-suicide endings of ménages à trois, not to mention the innumerable less traumatic but more common miseries afflicting human sexual life. Pessimism reminds us of its indispensable rule of thumb: experience is the only guide, hope can be a dangerous enemy.

14

GET REAL:
PESSIMISH AND TRAGEDY

> Poetry, said Santayana ... is "religion which is no longer be-
> lieved," but it depends, nevertheless, upon its power to revive in
> us a sort of temporary or provisional credence; and the nearer it
> can come to producing an illusion of belief, the greater its power
> as poetry. Once the Tragic Spirit was a living faith and out of it
> tragedies were written. Today these great expressions of a great
> faith have declined. Not merely into poetry, but into a kind of
> poetry whose premises are so far from any we can really accept
> that we can only partially and dimly grasp its meaning.
>
> We read but we do not write tragedies. The tragic solution of
> the problem of existence, the reconciliation to life by means of
> the tragic spirit is ... now only a fiction surviving in art.
>
> —Joseph Wood Krutch, *The Modern Temper* (1929)

The word "tragedy" has undergone a notable devolution in recent years. It's now routinely used to refer to any death whatsoever or even any sad event, like a romantic break-up, as in the Bee Gees' amusingly inane song "Tragedy." Purists may wax indignant, hearing a term that belongs in discussions of Orestes, Oedipus, and Medea applied to, say, a loss in the NBA finals. But the more one looks at it, "tragedy" in the strict sense refers to a rare cultural creation, which even at its profoundest and most brilliant moments was always intellectually dubious, and which is now extinct. So why not dust it off and put it to less exalted uses?

In its first appearance, the work of Aeschylus, tragedy dealt with the most grisly and nightmarish of human actions (patricide, human sacrifice, cannibalism, etc.), only to show divine justice triumphing in the end. Tragedy made the outlandish visionary claim that despite the bloody chaos of human experience, there was a grand moral plan behind it all. As the chorus sings in *Agamemnon:*

> But Righteousness shines out
> from grimy dwellings, honoring
> the man who lives in virtue.
> She turns her eyes away
> from gold-encrusted mansions
> where men's hands are black,
> and moves towards integrity,
> rejecting power and wealth,
> which, though praised, are counterfeit.
> Righteousness leads all things
> to well-deserved fulfillment
>
>   —tr. Ian Johnston

Talk about a spectacularly counter-factual claim. Perhaps Aeschylus was driven to such wrong-headed optimism by exhilaration over the defeat of the Persian invasion of Greece. (Even Aeschylus, however, can't come up with any consoling thoughts about the death of Iphigeneia or the warriors at Troy.) Sophocles doesn't seem to have matched Aeschylus' "faith," but he still shows that, even if it involves a kind of overkill, the gods, by means of human agents, take control (eventually) of the human scene and straighten things out. As he writes in *Antigone*:

> The best part of happiness is prudence.
> *Never* act impiously toward the gods.
> Mighty words from the arrogant bring
> Mighty blows from the avenging gods.
> And thus they teach old men to be prudent.

But once again this really is too good to be true. The old man in this case happens to be Creon, and his road to wisdom is so brutally painful that it's hard to imagine him surviving more than a few days after the play ends. Laius is dead, killed by the son he never wanted to have. Jocasta is dead, killed by her own hand. Eteocles and Polyneices are dead, killed by one another. Oedipus is dead, with his miraculously pain-free extinction supposedly compensating for half a lifetime of horror. Haemon and

Antigone have slain themselves in despair; and Creon knows he bears much of the responsibility. And the gods couldn't do any better than this?

For his part, Euripides would have nothing to do with such piety. He takes the formula of hubris punished (what else was tragedy all about?) and shoves it down our throat. His gods (Aphrodite in *Hippolytus*, Dionysus in *The Bacchae*, Apollo in *Alcestis*) are no better than humans; in fact they're considerably worse—just as mean as we are, but far more powerful. The corpses of their admittedly imperfect, but savagely persecuted victims lie everywhere; and the notion of justice triumphant is presented only to be trashed. The same century that saw the emergence of the religious fantasy of tragedy saw its cynical profanation and rejection.

By the time of Shakespeare tragedy had really gone downhill. Krutch touts *Othello* as an example of a tragic grandeur that is now beyond our cultural reach—we can appreciate it, though not duplicate it—but he ignores serious problems with the play's unreflecting sexism. Would it have been o.k. for Othello to kill Desdemona if she HAD been committing adultery with Cassio? Apart from that issue, Shakespeare's tragedies are sensational explosions of beauty destroyed and heartbreaking loss; but they all posit a crew of idealized human specimens, and they all end with dubious affirmations of order (i.e., firm Patriarchal control) restored and hopeful new beginnings. It's fabulous poetry, but feeble philosophy.

At any rate, ancient and Renaissance tragedies share a belief in the heroic possibilities of humans (which usually means men) that for a number of reasons moderns simply can't accept. In a democratic age we can't take kings and princes seriously as any more different from us than the rich. Heroes were originally demigods, the offspring of divine fathers or mothers and human mates. That's gone forever. In an age of genocide and democide we see individual destinies as shrunken and less significant (if people want to indulge in the luxury of private passions and tragic flaws that cause their own death or downfall, fine, let them). We have a hard time believing that wisdom, or anything else of value, comes through suffering; e.g., whatever lessons may be learned from the Holocaust are horrifically disproportionate to its cost. What wisdom emerged from 9/11? What would Aeschylus or Shakespeare have done with AIDS? We see no reason to think that a family bloodbath can "purge" a festering evil and restore the state—or anything else.

Tragedy, it turns out, is a sort of delicious moral fantasy, masochism at its most sublime. A little willing suspension of disbelief; and we're off. St. Augustine, that crazed puritan, was right to suspect the motives of readers or audiences of tragic tales: they may have been weeping, but they were plainly enjoying themselves. Pessimism tells us that enjoying the show is all right—just don't try to take any consoling messages home with you. And abandon the luxury of "the tragic sense of life"—save it for those who die young and their grieving survivors.

Once more, look at some of Shakespeare's tragedies. Romeo and Juliet were just hormone-crazed teenagers (as we can see in the farcical version of the double suicide of Pyramus and Thisbe in *A Midsummer's Night Dream*). Hamlet should have returned to graduate school in Wittenberg, stayed out of politics, and let his mother resolve her sexual issues. Othello should have gone to marriage counseling (and he should have thought twice about robbing the cradle). More than anything else Lear needed a shrink and Prozac (besides, monarchy's a bad idea, as Macbeth discovered). This is aestheticized agony at its finest—but that means it's real art and fake agony (with "picturesque" deaths, eloquent parting words, and, almost always, the social order still firmly in place).

And so on. In a world as bloodied and battered as ours, we can't afford the antics of these spoiled aristocrats, except on the stage; and there's a limit to how much we can get worked up over them. Medea just needed an equitable divorce, as did Anna Karenina. Emma Bovary and Tess of the D'Urbervilles needed scholarships to Oxford or Wellesley. The appeal of what Krutch calls "the tragic fallacy" is obvious (even as we can't miss its fallaciousness). Life never stops giving us lemons, so why not make champagne-quality lemonade out of them? Suffering makes a more interesting spectacle than happiness (we rubberneck at the scene of a car crash, not of a quiet family picnic), so the more suffering, the better. The ancient Greeks thought the gods were jealous of anybody with godlike gifts or pretensions; *we* certainly envy such people, and watching anyone with a high profile suffer is a delicious source of *Schadenfreude*, if nothing else. And throw in all the other familiar clichés: misery loves company, good news is no news, it's pleasant to watch the distress of others from a safe distance; even Murphy's law could be seen as a sort of tragic formula.

In the end you can't have tragedy without very high expectations (of life, of human beings, of the cosmos, etc.), and because it's intent on lowering expectations, pessimism is anti-tragic. People will surely go on using the word, but its true sense no longer applies. The world we live in simply can't support tragedy. It isn't, one might say, good enough for tragedy. Every time we say the word, we'll have to take a quick mental discount.

No matter, we have a plentiful supply of more accurate words, ranging from sad and disappointing to horrible and catastrophic. And the world will go supplying us with experiences to attach these labels to—while the gods forever fail to intervene and set things right, except in the *Eumenides* (where their decision to save the day by making Clytemnestra a non-person is highly suspect). Nowadays the only thing a honest tragic chorus could do, most of the time anyhow, is weep and curse.

15

ANYBODY HOME?
PESSIMISM IN A CHAOTIC
COSMOS

The starry order in which we live is an exception; this order and
the relative permanence conditioned by it has again made
possible the exception of exceptions: the formation of the
organic. The overall character of the world is, however, to all
eternity chaos, not in the sense that necessity is lacking but that
order, organization, form, beauty, wisdom and all our human
aesthetic notions are lacking.

—Nietzsche, *The Gay Science*

One of the ultimate definers of a culture is what it habitually says in
the face of death. You could get a quick overview of English life,
thought, and art by comparing Milton's *Lycidas* (1638) with Johnson's *On
the Death of Dr. Robert Levet* (1783), Shelley's *Adonais* (1821), Tenny-
son's *In Memoriam* (1850), Arnold's *Thyrsis* (1866) and W.H. Auden's *In
Memory of W.B. Yeats* (1939), and noting how much less each succeeding
elegy was able to affirm.

In a similar vein, one of the sure signs of the progressive weakening of
Christianity is the feeble-futile eulogies one hears nowadays at Christian
funerals. In my Catholic childhood (1940s-1950s) there were no eulogies
at funerals; the liturgy, presumably, said all that needed to be said. The fact
that more words have to be added could in itself seem suspicious. Does
God's action in "taking" the departed (or in not preventing him or her from
being "taken") suddenly need justification? The preacher sounds defensive.

Nowadays even Christian clergymen have adopted the "We're not mourning the death, we're celebrating the life" mode, as if to admit that there was nothing comforting in death.

Actually, theodicy has always been the weakest part of Christian dogma. (The word itself isn't often heard nowadays; there's "apologetics," but that has unintended connotations.) The validity of religion, it would seem, should be taken for granted in a religious society. Once believers have to begin explaining their position to, and defending it against, other people (and, worse yet, themselves), something has obviously gone wrong. Building the Great Wall of China was not a sign of strength. The most famous piece of apologetics in modern literature, Pascal's unfinished *Pensées*, is mostly remembered, not for its devout sockdolagers, but for the haunting lines Pascal puts in the mouth of his wretched, but honest *libertin* ("The last act is bloody, however fine the rest of the play. In the end they throw dirt over your head, and that's it forever," etc.)

The simple fact is that theism, Christian, Jewish, or Muslim, doesn't fare very well in the court of secular reason. The Book of Job stuns us with its alternating heart-wrenching and thunderous poetry, not with any convincing account it gives of "why bad things happen to good people." The Bible itself (as in the Book of Jeremiah and elsewhere) allows Jobian-complainers to vent their pain and fury on God; but it offers no intellectual solutions to the problem. (How could it? If there were any such solution, someone would have figured it out long ago.)

Proponents of so-called process theology take the reasonable step of backing away from an absolutely perfect, completely "finished," omnipotent, omniscient, etc. Supreme Being and opting for a God still under development. ("Cut God a break," one imagines them saying, "he's doing the best he can.") This at least provides a better fit for our experience of the world and history as terribly messy, but it jettisons millennia of the sort of God-talk most people are used to.

As ever, the problem of evil is the killer. Schopenhauer pithily sums this up when he writes: "But the idea that a god like *Jehovah* produces this world of distress and woe *animi causa* [on a whim] and *de gaieté de coeur* [with merry heart] and then actually proceeds to applaud himself for it, saying *panta kala lian* (it is all very good), that is unbearable" (*Parerga and Paralipomena*, 156). Perhaps from God's fancy executive suite high in heaven he can't see (or foresee) all the plagues, tortures, and butcheries that fill our headlines.

Technically, in the Pauline-Augustinian-Lutheran, etc. view, whatever goes wrong here below can be blamed on sin (Adam's *Erbsünde* and his children's moral lapses); but this is too prima facie preposterous to merit a response—other than to say that, like most theistic teachings, it completely ignores the life, suffering, and death of non-moral animals.

In any case, beyond the hopelessly tangled issue of responsibility for our dolorous condition in this, as the *Salve, Regina* calls it, vale of tears, lies the larger, and absolutely unending, dispute over any kind of order in the cosmos. (Insofar as the universe can be compared to a classroom or an office) is anyone or anything in charge? The preponderance of the evidence says no. Nietzsche's response in *The Gay Science* (109) is emphatic: "How can we venture to reprove or praise the universe? Let us beware of attributing to it heartlessness and unreason or their opposites: it is neither perfect nor beautiful nor noble, and has no desire to become any of these; it is by no means striving to imitate mankind! It is quite impervious to all our aesthetic and moral judgments! It has likewise no impulse to self-preservation or impulses of any kind; neither does it know any laws. Let us beware of saying there are any laws in nature. There are only necessities: there is no one to command, no one to obey, no one to transgress. When you realize that there are no goals or objectives, then you realize, too, that there is no chance: for only in a world of objectives does the word 'chance' have any meaning. "

Can't we even say "randomness"? Nietzsche seems to be setting the bar too high. Oh well. But even if the naïve old images of a Heavenly Father (Michelangelo's, for instance) look useless even to thoughtful believers nowadays, there's something appealing in Milton's vision of Chaos in *Paradise Lost*:

> When straight behold the throne
> Of Chaos, and his dark pavilion spread
> Wide on the wasteful deep; with him enthroned
> Sat sable-vested Night, eldest of things
> … and him [Satan] thus the anarch old
> With faltering speech and visage incomposed
> Answered: (II, 959-62, 988-990)

If we can't have the *Rex tremendae majestatis*—and we can't: no one judge could handle the gigantic backlog of cases on the Doomsday docket, and who wants a king nowadays?—a figure like Milton's zonked-out Chaos or the crazed, babbling Orator at the end of Ionesco's *The Chairs* (1952) seems right for the world as we know it. We can *say* things like, "In the time it takes to read this sentence, the universe will increase in volume by

100 trillion cubic light-years" (Terence Dickinson, *Nightwatch*), but how can we possibly imagine *that*, since light travels about a million times faster than the fastest thing we've ever experienced, a jet plane? What sense can we make of the statement that there are likely something like 50 billion galaxies in the universe when most of us have only the flimsiest grasp of our own galaxy? And what to think of all that useless celestial real estate, where "[There is] less than one atom for every cubic centimeter, compared with ten million trillion atoms per cubic centimeter of air at sea level on Earth" (Terence Dickinson)? So, having an "anarch" who is (not) in charge of this incomprehensibly vast and mostly empty space sounds fitting.

Such reflections might not necessarily give birth to pessimism, or not just to pessimism. Astonishment, awe, bewilderment, confusion, terror, delight would all be understandable, if not inevitable, reactions. And one could even break out into pantheistic Whitmanesque hallelujahs ("And a mouse is miracle enough to stagger sextillions of infidels") at the enormous show. But knowing that the universe isn't our "home" in the usual *gemütlich* sense of the term, that it "cuts us down to size," that we can never plumb its depths nor reach its frontiers (what would lie beyond?), that, whatever the truth about the Big Bang, the universe can never end, while *we*'ll be finished in the twinkling of an eye, that the whole sprawling mass just "happened," without rhyme or reason—all that appears to, at the least, give the lie to optimism.

Earth is like a leaky ocean liner, minus captain and crew, sailing a limitless ocean. There's no destination, known or unknown; and the passengers have forgotten, if they ever knew, why they got on board in the first place. Meanwhile the "burials at sea" continue apace. (Of course, none of this need trouble the Stoic, *if* one can be a Stoic. "Let a man once overcome his selfish terror at his one finitude," said George Santayana in *The Ethics of Spinoza* (1910), "and his finitude is, in one sense overcome." Nice work if you can get it.)

From Nietzsche's point of view, the anarchy of the universe gets us all off the hook: no one is responsible for anything because we are all a part of everything, which has no rhyme or reason except insofar as we project them into the universe (because we can't help doing so). Well, for Nietzsche, with his Lutheranism-plagued boyhood (and for anyone else inoculated with the poison of theism), this may have been a welcome liberation. Nonetheless, it leaves a certain gap. Pessimism tells us that we just have to go on living (well, we don't actually *have to*) with it. Accept the evidence; relax and, if possible, enjoy the ride. Unfortunately, that line has been used before—by rapists, for example. *C'est dommage* (which some might see as the cry of pessimists everywhere). Unlike various kinds of philosophical defense-mechanisms, pessimism directly tackles one of the basic facts of the human condition: that we live in a world of unsettling, even terrifying, flux.

At some pivotal point in his life, Galileo supposedly muttered, "E pur si muove"—It (the earth) does too move. Did he say this, as legend has it, just after kneeling and submitting to the Inquisition to save his life? Or later when leaving house arrest in Siena? In either event he couldn't say it out loud; and even today, though no longer controversial, the idea is still unsettling.

Apart from their naive approach to the Bible, Galileo's examiners had a hard time believing in heliocentrism because it flies in the face of everyday experience: except for the terrifying jolt of earthquakes, the earth, thank God, stands perfectly still. Bodies of water generally don't: after a stomach-churning sea voyage we're all glad to be back on *terra firma*. The more *firma*, an old joke says, the less *terra*.

Well, everyone's who's been to college, or at least watched *Jeopardy*, knows that Heraclitus said, "All things flow, nothing stays put"; and no one has ever refuted him. But that's not how it feels. The earth may be spinning on its axis at 1,000 miles an hour and in its orbit around the sun at 67 times faster than that, but diamond cutters and brain surgeons on the job never lift an eyebrow. The illusion of stability is so strong that Galileo's point has to be made emphatically. *Everything* moves, but we constantly delude ourselves into thinking the opposite. Consider what could be called the photographic, the narrative, and the linguistic illusion.

We are all fooled by "snapshots." Photographic images are so hypnotizing that we forget how false they are. Every now and then the quirks of lighting and posing create so distorted an image of, for instance, ourselves that we protest: We don't look like *that*. And we're right, of course; but we don't look exactly like any other image of ourselves either. Nevertheless we take pictures with either film or brain cells and stubbornly carry them around in our wallets or heads. Then time passes, and we get brought up short—at a school reunion, for example—by the contrast between an old image of somebody or something and the new reality (or rather a new image). All our images are clichés (literally a stereotype-plate or negative) that try to fix protean reality with a few crude simplifying strokes, as do verbal clichés like sunny California, dirty dishwater, or Slick Willy.

The narrative illusion can be easily observed on the nightly news: a few facts (or factoids) and video clips stitched together (perhaps with a backdrop shot of the Capitol for authenticity) to form a *story* are presented as the essential developments in the world since we last checked. There are so many fallacies in all this that we can hardly, as the proverb says, shake a stick at them. First, a staggering, inconceivable number and variety of movements are reduced to a laughably tiny selection. Then they get frozen and stuffed into a convenient, but fictitious narrative package with an Aristotelean beginning, middle, and (at least provisional) end. As Sartre argues in *Nausea* (1938), we tell all our stories backwards, with the meaningful conclusion present but hidden in the beginning. The narrator knows and controls this shell game; the careful reader, or re-reader, can follow it; but at the time the protagonist, real or imagined, didn't and couldn't see the pattern, because it wasn't there yet.

All narrative beginnings, as Sartre points out, are falsified: "There I was," we say, "strolling down the street, without a care in the world. And then, all of a sudden ... " It sounds fine, but the "all of a sudden"—like the staccato, threatening ruffle of drums in a movie score when the innocent hero enters a dimly lit room where the murderer is lurking—transforms the original moment and makes it pregnant with a scary interest that it never had.

Stories wade into the helter-skelter confusion of lived experience like a mother into her children's room, and "clean it up," i.e., make it esthetically pleasant by imposing order on it. Once again, we are so taken with the results that we don't quarrel or quibble with the cheating that has taken place. Out of the vast flood of experience, the narrator has scooped a bucketful and presented it for our admiration: What a nice pail! What sparkling water! Meanwhile the river of history (the source of all stories), which, unlike real rivers, has no fixed bed, which arises and empties out no one knows where, flows murkily and aimlessly on.

The narrative illusion always overstresses endings, because we can't understand anything without closure. Whence the two-minute warning in pro football and the exaggerated attention paid to the last few seconds of all clock-driven games (as if all the preceding, "undramatic" seconds and plays were not equally determinative of the final score). The "buzzer-beater" is no more important, mathematically, than any of the other baskets, made or not made, in the course of the game. But that's not how we see it or feel it.

Perhaps the key to all this is the linguistic illusion: humans have built language as their way of inhabiting the world. It's amazingly comfortable and convenient, a palace in fact (compared with the meager—we presume—symbolic caves and dens of animals, who don't even have color TV); but it's also a prison, and we all serve a life sentence in it. Language works so well that it suckers us into hypostatization, the mistaking of words for things. In Genesis 2 Adam makes up names for all his fellow creatures—including his wife—and thereby "gets a handle" on them. (An alienating process, being named and defined by somebody else, though it happens to every one us.)

But the handiness of labels (multiplied by the millions) leads us to believe that a) the "contents" we paste them on are stable and b) that we know all about them. Scanning a face in a crowd we say, "Oh, I know him, that's Joe Blow." But how much do we know of Joe Blow beyond a handful of vague impressions? And, even if we knew 100,000 times more about him than we do, is Joe Blow some kind of rigid, immobile essence. *E pur si muove!*

Everybody does this all the time. We try to reduce the continuous flow of reality to graspable conceptual cubes ("a bonehead play," "a brilliant move," "a new arrangement"). We fuse the scattered fragments of experience into outrageously sloppy generalizations ("a good time," "a bad neighborhood," "a big country"). We invent linguistic tokens and counters—and then trade with them for all they're worth. In fact people, or at least men, often wind up killing other people with the "wrong" ethnic, racial, religious, or tribal ID's. In the Book of Judges (12.6) 42,000 men are slaughtered because they can't pronounce the "sh" in "shibboleth" correctly. "Don't move, or I'll shoot," guards shout at intruders—and something is always intruding on our fixed little universe.

We are, it seems, drunk on our fantasies of an unchanging, unmoving world. And no wonder: all our illusions, photographic narrative, and linguistic, are so intoxicating. They don't just reflect the world, they make things happen. Words and pictures, artfully combined and efficiently applied, can get us from here to there, can pack the shelves of the Library of Congress, can erect the Pantheon or blow up Hiroshima. They help us negotiate, and make sense of, our universe.

The only problem is, they're all basically deceptive. They're only snapshots (*instantanés* the French call them), not movies (and movies themselves are only 24 snapshots a second). We could live happily ever after with our illusions, if only we didn't periodically get flashes of stomach-turning turbulence: Whoa, this baby (the ground beneath our feet, our bodies, the whole planet) is moving. And not just moving: shifting, turning, spinning, crashing, growing, living, dying. "Stop the world, I want to get off!" someone with motion sickness shouts. Our conductor and fellow passenger, Galileo Galilei, looks over at Heraclitus, smiles, and shakes his head. There is, of course, a kind of Dramamine for this condition: pessimism. Taken regularly, it can provide at least a modicum of relief. Try it.

16

YOU THINK *YOU* GOT TBOUBLE: PROVERBIAL PESSIMISM

Altsding lozt zich ois mit a gevain. [Everything ends in tears.]

—Yiddish proverb

The pessimistic depths of Jewish literature are vast. The Bible, to begin with, is an angry book. Three-quarters of all prophetic oracles, it has been calculated, are negative: furious, though (or precisely for that reason) often seemingly hopeless tirades against evildoers, idolaters, etc. Not much constructive criticism here. The Old Testament prophets—and John the Baptist and Jesus in their wake—constantly speak in sweeping negatives. The prophets don't EVER say things like, "A large minority of my people have gone astray," or "Perhaps as many as 78% of the local population are occasionally guilty of social injustice."

Instead they issue ferocious, take-no-prisoners tirades: "The ox knoweth his owner, and the ass his master's crib; but Israel doth not know, my people doth not consider. Ah, sinful nation, a people laden with iniquity, a seed of evildoers, children that are corrupters; they have forsaken the LORD; they have provoked the Holy One of Israel unto anger" (Is. 1.3-4). Not for nothing is Jeremiah credited with inventing his own querulous genre. "For from the least of them even unto the greatest of them," he writes in 6.13, "every one is given to covetousness; and from the prophet even unto the priest every one dealeth falsely." *Every one.*

But the prophets aren't half the story. Prophecy, after all, eventually vanished as a genre. As Israel lost, first its territorial integrity (722 BCE) and then (587 BCE) its independence, and plunged into endless oppressive travails, the last thing Jews needed was a bunch of nagging or blistering national critics. Still, the one part of life that wouldn't go away was history (the Tanakh ends with Chronicles, not, like the Christian Old Testament, with the prophet Malachi); and the Bible's take on Jewish history is a masterpiece of self-criticism, if not self-hatred.

There was, admittedly, a sort of honeymoon period in the days of the patriarchs. Beginning with the flight of Abraham from Haran in northwest Mesopotamia (Gen. 12) to the "birth of the nation" in the crossing of the Red Sea (Ex. 14) the behavior of the "Founding Fathers" is not especially admirable (both Abraham and Isaac gutlessly hand their wives over to more powerful men); but the storytellers, whoever they are, don't seem to be troubled by that. After the arrival in the Sinai, however, the Bible has little else to talk about but failure for six hundred years or so.

True, the Book of Joshua presents a loathsomely triumphalist account of how the Israelites smashed the Canaanites and conquered their new home. But the book ends, as Deuteronomy before it does, with the Commander-in-Chief casting a baleful eye on a future that he *knows* will be disastrous ("You cannot serve the LORD; for he is a holy God; he is a jealous God; he will not forgive your transgressions or your sins" Jos. 24.19). From Exodus down through Ezra and Nehemiah, the message of Israel's "historians" is excruciating simple: We (and our forefathers) blew it. No sooner had the Israelites escaped from Egypt than they began murmuring against Moses and wishing they had never left (whence the corny old joke about the Jew weeping at the Western Wall: "My people, I want to be with my people!" Bystander: "What do you mean? This is Israel, you *are* with your people." Wailer: "My people are in Miami!")

Throughout the history of ancient Israel there was constant internal conflict and even bloody civil war, as seen in the Book of Judges. The kings were almost all bad; and even the good ones (David, Solomon, Josiah) are seen doing things that strike a modern reader as dubious if not despicable (assassinations, trickery, etc.). In any case the kingdoms of the North (Israel) and the South (Judah) were destroyed; and the House of David never made the successful return that the prophets in their more sanguine moments liked to dream about. One sometimes can make out in the Bible itself an uneasiness over all this negativity; for example, the Books of Chronicles air-brush away some embarrassing material, such as David's adultery with Bathsheba and his ruthless, godfather-like advice to Solomon about whacking Joab and Shimei after he dies. Not for nothing are Jews famous for guilt.

Of course, there's a ready secular explanation for this non-stop badmouthing. If we assume that the Jews began assembling their historical or quasi-historical narratives only during and after the catastrophe of the Babylonian Exile (587-538 BCE), then it would seem reasonable to find a bitter bias in the story. Since God rewards those who keep the Law and punishes those who break it, then the unspeakable hard times Israel went through must, logically, have been its own fault. True, the Talmud abandoned this relentless guilt-trip (and the mere thought of applying it to the Holocaust is horrific); but Jewish tradition never came up with a similarly compelling story. So Jews (and Bible-believing Christians) are stuck with this inescapable pessimism: we are worse than the heathens. For example, the brutal mob of homosexual rapists from Gibeah in Judges 19 imitates and then outdoes the Sodomites in Genesis 19 (who never actually raped anyone).

Fast-forward to 20th and 21st century America, where by a twist of fate the kings of comedy turned out to be, in massive disproportion to their numbers, Jews. From the Marx Brothers to Jerry Seinfeld and Larry David, it's a familiar story. Perhaps Jewish comedians provided the necessary outlet for negatives that couldn't be found in the sunny clime of America's fatuous official optimism.

In any case the world of Jewish-American humor is too big for a quick fly-over. But perhaps a look at Yiddish proverbs, which certainly capture the environment out of which American Jewish culture, and not just its humor, grew, can illustrate the nature of Jewish pessimism.

A survey of some popular Yiddish proverbs clarifies a number of points that might at first blush seem odd, if not unsettling , in a traditionally pious culture. For starters, in this supposedly God-centered universe God himself gets judged rather harshly. "If God ever lived on earth, people would smash in all his windows." One even occasionally hears a note that sounds like outright impiety. "If praying to God did any good, they'd hire people to do it." In the harsh Jew-hating world most Yiddish speakers lived in, God was an august but faraway presence. God, as the Book of Job flatly asserts, is ungraspable. Or, as the rhyming Yiddish proverb says, "der mentsh tracht un got lacht"—"Man plans and God laughs." Not only do the best-laid plans of mice and men gang oft agley, God goes out of his way to derail them.

Despite the intense community ties (and utter lack of privacy) in the shtetl, Yiddish proverbs stress isolation and everyman for himself. It may be true that, "One does not perish among Jews"; but you can come pretty close to it. After all, "A friend remains a friend until you get to his pockets." You laugh alone and you cry alone." "A stranger's troubles aren't worth an onion." "A boil is o.k. so long as it's under somebody else's arm" (or, as Mel Brooks likes to say, "Tragedy is when I cut my finger, comedy is when you fall into a ditch and die.") "The world is full of troubles, but all anyone feels is his own." While The Ethics of the Fathers, the great tractate in the Mishna, piously claims that, "The World rests on three pillars: on the Torah, on serving God, and on works of charity" (1,1), a defiant Yiddish proverb responds with a mocking rhyme of "velt" and "gelt": "The world rests on three things: money, money, and money."

Money, of course, is what most Jews greatly lacked; and Yiddish proverbs, unlike Christian preachers, refuse to "spiritualize" or idealize this cruel fact. "The wife weeps and the dog howls, the baby whimpers and poverty bangs away." "You know who comes out to honor a pauper? A cold wind and a vicious dog." "May God bless me so I won't need people." (So much for Barbra Streisand's insufferable, schmaltzy refrain that, "People who need people are the luckiest people in the world." (No wonder she was so unconvincing as "Yentl, the Yeshiva Boy.") "All of life is a war."

Christianity may idealize the "fool for Christ," but the sharpest digs of Yiddish proverbs are saved for fools: in a Darwinian struggle for existence in a Jew-hating world, thoughtlessness is a fatal luxury. "A fool loses and a smart guy finds." "A fool enters the bath and forgets to wash his feet." "Fools don't need rain to grow." We might note that the fool's moral status (like the rich man's) is irrelevant. This takes us back to the fundamentally secular Book of Proverbs, where Israelite scribes borrowed from Egyptian and Assyrian sources to supply ambitious young men with advice for negotiating their way through the jungle of the professional world. (That tradition shares with Yiddish proverbs a misogynistic bias, seeing women mostly as a source of trouble and temptation.)

The big difference is that the environment of the Yiddish proverbs is much more threatening. "So many Hamans and only one Purim." And its variant, "Only one God and so many enemies." And the laconic observation that, "When the goyim have a celebration, they beat up Jews."

The only remedy for these and other evils—the only verbal remedy at any rate—is a batch of comic devices: irony, sarcasm, self-mockery. "If you don't want to get old, hang yourself while you're young."

Other proverbs explain this process. "You can't change the world—not with curses and not with laughter." But both provide (temporary) relief; and so, "A bitter heart never shuts up." What it speaks is the language of pessimism. "Life is like a child's jacket—short and dirty." On the other hand, that doesn't stop people from clinging to it. "Life is just a dream, but don't wake me up." Another proverb, which addresses the sort of awkward objects we all have around the house but just can't get rid of, might be talking about life itself: "It's too heavy to carry, but you're sorry to throw it away."

It's a curious feature of the so-called "wisdom literature" in the Bible, that two of the three members of that genre (Job and Ecclesiastes, with its irreligious refrain that "All is futility") could be described as subversive in that they raise serious questions about divine justice. But even the generally staid and conservative Book of Proverbs sometimes rates honest realism over moral principle: "A bribe is like a magic stone in the eyes of him who gives it; wherever he turns he prospers" (17.8). "The rich rules over the poor, and the borrower is the slave of the lender" (22.7). Though usually hostile to alcohol, Proverbs advises, "Give strong drink to him who is perishing, and wine to those in bitter distress" (31.6). Where God won't help, you look to whatever gets you through the night. The Sages have no objection to that.

The editorial principle that admitted such unpleasant thoughts into the biblical canon (along with other far more radical ones, like Ecclesiastes' "Be not righteous overmuch" [7.16]) may have been something like, "Well, this is just a one-liner; it adds a little variety; why not?" In any case, such broad license for cognitive dissonance is one of the things that make the Hebrew Bible more enjoyable than the theologically "straighter" New Testament.

And Yiddish proverbs carry on this legacy of tough, unedifying "zingers." "The Torah shines, the Torah burns, but only cash keeps you warm." "The grave is already open (*shoin ofen*), and they go on hoping (*tut noch hofen*)." The point of such trouble-making pessimism is that, like the continuously negative, complaining, self-pitying and self-mocking strains of American Jewish humor, in the final analysis it makes you feel better. Pessimism is a form of comic relief. Out with it, Yiddish proverbs seem to be saying, out with the worst of it—so we can face it and move on. Pessimism, strangely enough, is good for you.

17

THINGS AREN'T *THAT* BAD: SILLY PESSIMISM

> In early youth we sit before our future like children sitting before the curtain in a theatre, in cheerful, eager expectation of the play about to be shown. How fortunate that we don't know what really will come. Those who do know may see children as innocent offenders, sentenced, not to death but to life, as prisoners who have yet to hear the terms of their sentence.—Nevertheless, everyone wants to reach a ripe old age, in other words a state where they will say: "It's bad today, it will get worse with each succeeding day—until the very worst arrives."
>
> —Arthur Schopenhauer, *Parerga and Paralipomena*, 155

If anything could give pessimism a bad name, it's pessimists. But the term is often used sloppily: hard-nosed realists, acerbic critics, Swiftian misanthropists, soppy wet-blankets, cartoonish Jewish mothers, Chicken Little prophets of doom, and so forth are all likely to be labeled "pessimists" by "positive thinkers." One of the older journalistic clichés is to mock the turn-of-the 20th-century editorialists who thought the streets of New York were about to disappear under chest-high piles of horse manure (not realizing that they—and all of us—were going to be "saved" by the carbon-spewing horseless carriage). Nowadays the growing consensus that there is no technological solution for our ecological woes is putting a damper on such prospects for a happy surprise.

"Pessimist" would be better used to apply to thinkers like Plato, St. Paul, Augustine, Pascal, and others (Schopenhauer on a bad day), whose views of life are needlessly, at times even grotesquely, negative. Such writers are, typically, misogynistic, ascetical, and blind or hostile to the pleasures and sweetness of the passing moment. Anyone who claims that real life is "somewhere else," in whatever super-terrestrial sphere(s), that the flesh is a distraction, and that women are to be feared (and therefore hated) is a pessimist in the worst sense.

Surely one of the sillier forms of theological pessimism is the doctrine of sin. It's worth spending some time on, because it's at once a very popular and a very bad explanation for the miseries of life. Asked about a sermon on sin he'd just heard, Calvin Coolidge could recall only that the preacher was against it. Other Christian spokesmen, however, before and since, have been more expansive on the subject: just turn on any Christian channel. If you want to get really dizzy, read the 20,000-or-so-word article on "Sin" ("human deviation from the expressed will and desire of God") in the *Anchor Bible Dictionary*: it's as dense and demanding as a final exam in biochemistry.

Well, let's try a shortcut through this desiccated jungle, and begin by assuming that there is a God who has in fact plainly expressed his or her "will and desire," and that human beings, for whatever reason, perversely or otherwise, "deviate" from this will, thereby becoming sinners. We may leave aside, for the moment anyhow, the question of how sin differs from a non-religious notion of harm done to oneself or other creatures. We may likewise accept without challenge the theological axiom that we are all sinners. Finally, if we acknowledge that sin has anything to do with the deplorable state of the world, now or at any other time, we can agree that sin *is* dreadful, and that anyone who could do anything to lessen its frequency or mitigate its effects would deserve universal applause.

Here, of course, is where Christianity comes in: Jesus died, we are told, to save us from our sins (Romans 5.18, etc.) Thanks to his mysterious sacrifice, the "Lamb of God" took away the sins of the world. In many ways, this is a highly dubious idea: how does the death of an innocent man erase the moral responsibility of billions of other people (the majority of whom have never heard of him)? Does an action that was itself a crime get rid of previous and future crimes? Does Jesus' blood (a drop in the literal ocean of blood unjustly shed throughout history) miraculously turn into an endlessly spouting geyser to wipe clean the gigantic (and still expanding) slate of millennia of crimes and cruelties? The crazy pessimism of sin leads to the ludicrous, utopian optimism of redemption.

The usual doctrines of redemption are incredibly far-fetched: an infinite offense (Adam and Eve's disobedience) against an infinite being (God) could be removed only by the sacrifice of an infinite being, who was by nature both (how neat is this?!) a member of the offending species *and* the injured party himself. Then, of course, we have original sin and individual sins, venial sins and mortal sins, and the underlying assumption that humans are free enough to be tried and found guilty in the court of heaven for whatever they do. (Pessimism, of course, says that all this is nonsense: our woes are essentially incurable, and there is no redemption to be looked for.)

These issues have worried theologians for centuries, but let's skip over them and assume further that Jesus did indeed win us pardon for our sins. There is at least no doubt that "sin" is a handy category, a broad label for things we hate, that hurt ourselves and others. These things might well be seen as incurring the condemnation of a higher power; and humans often feel personally and subjectively guilty for having done them. Suppose we could whisk away any divine displeasure and assure ourselves that somehow the status of our action had changed, as if an enormous debt had been paid or gratuitously canceled. What then?

Well, we might (and some of us do) feel enormously relieved, but the world would not have changed very much; because sin doesn't serve as a very useful explanation or description of the pains, troubles, sufferings, and horror sometimes referred to as the human condition. How much "sin" was involved in dropping the atomic bomb on Hiroshima and Nagasaki? The leading American agents of this disaster, from Harry Truman to the pilots of the *Enola Gay*, all thought of themselves as acting virtuously; and given the state of the world at the time, etc., it's hard to see how they could have thought otherwise. Naturally, we'd never accept the same excuse for members of the SS and other agents of Hitler's "Final Solution"; and many of us would agree that far more Nazis should have been tried, condemned, and hanged at Nuremberg.

But would their "sins," their consciously evil choices, provide an intelligible account of the unspeakable suffering that these men unleashed? (For one last time, note that men commit the overwhelming majority of the really horrendous—or even just the historically "interesting"—sins. To call a woman a sinner [e.g., Luke 7.37] has almost always been code language for only one offence: her refusal to limit her sexual favors to her husband-owner.)

The picture is complicated by factors such as moral blindness, laziness, passivity, herd behavior, unfortunate timing, stupidity, and the countless structural flaws of human cultures and institutions. One can do terrible things, as Adolf Eichmann did, without having a Satanic moral stature. And technology can multiply a thousand times over the destructive power of an otherwise tiny individual. Under the "right" circumstances, a handful of drunken officers with the codes for firing nuclear missiles could wreak more havoc than the cruelest dictators and tyrants of world history to date, or at least until the mid-20th century. The devisers of such a system, its engineers and scientific and political inventors, would have a share in the guilt for the smoking ruins and the tens of millions of corpses that might result from such a lapse; but the precise moral state of the perpetrators' consciences would seem, all things considered, to be a rather trivial feature of the whole nightmarish picture.

How many "sins" were committed in the transmission and spread of the AIDS pandemic over the last twenty years? Any more than were committed during the same period on the floor of the New York Stock Exchange or in corporate boardrooms? The very worst thing that humans can do, generally speaking, is wage war. But do the guilty decisions, choices, and actions of the warring nations' leaders bear any sort of meaningful proportion to the harm they have unleashed? How many "sins" have been committed in the practice of clitoridectomy in Africa and beyond? How many conscious crimes were committed in the despoliation of the natural world, from the emergence of *homo sapiens* to global warming? (By some traditional methods of moral calculation the answer there would be none, since one cannot sin against inanimate nature.)

Once again, let's imagine that all this could be specified and quantified in the mind of God, and that all the sin involved could be cleared away. What ultimate good would that do? How much of the damage could be repaired? Can past agony be undone? Can the pain inflicted and lives destroyed (or species annihilated) be in any sense brought back? Pessimism, as always, insists on doing the math.

Sin appears to be a nearly useless category when it comes to the random suffering caused by cancer and other diseases, car crashes and other accidents (unless all that is in some sense a consequence of the "Fall"). The randomness and facticity of existence, the thousand natural shocks that flesh is heir to, likewise have no moral status. Theologians like to connect the supreme instance of human limitation, death, with sin; but this is problematic because animals, who are not moral agents (though they can inflict and feel pain) and presumably non-sentient plants die just as we do. Forces with no clear moral status—intelligence, cunning, or the lack of them, good fortune or misfortune, the refractoriness of matter—play an enormous and, in fact, preponderant role in our destiny and the happiness or unhappiness of our lives.

Finally, if sin—and the freedom needed to commit it—is real, what does God do about it? Nothing much, at least in the here and now, to judge by the many anguished complaints in the Bible, from Jeremiah to the Book of Job, not to mention the tormented cry in Ecclesiastes: "Again I saw all the oppressions that are practiced under the sun. And behold, the tears of the oppressed, and they had no one to comfort them! On the side of their oppressors there was power, and there was no one to comfort them" (Eccl.4 1-2).

The solution eventually devised to remedy this intolerable situation was, of course, the afterlife, with its punishments and rewards, the former a two-tiered system in Catholicism, with temporary purgation for lesser offenses and eternal torture for the unforgivable ones. Other than satisfying a divine need for vengeance, Hell appears to have no positive function at all; whereas Purgatory sounds, at first anyhow, somewhat rational. But every kind of punishment, terrestrial or otherwise, always causes headaches. Is suffering educational? What does "paying one's debt" (whether to society or God) accomplish? Could any system of exquisitely calibrated other-worldly punishments ever be thought up to "straighten out" sinners for good? Pessimism—and common sense—says no.

In the end "sin" proves to be a potent buzzword, but a dubious and primitive idea, pure fantasy parading as description. If everything the Christians tell us about it were true, we still wouldn't have learned very much about the real world. Perhaps the ultimate appeal of "sin" is its power to simplify things. Whereas evil is intolerably complex, an absolute tangle of over-determined forces (such as testosterone levels, military traditions, demented codes of "honor") and imponderable what-ifs (what if Sirhan Sirhan's aim had been worse? what if John Hinckley's had been better? what if men hadn't always oppressed women?)

Apart from its complexity, evil (which pessimism would define neutrally as anything that hurts) baffles us by its continuousness, its belonging to a seamless temporal and causal flow, like a strand in a vast web. "Sin," by contrast, can be understood as specific, discrete, freely chosen individual acts, for example, as items to be confessed to a priest. If sins are like debts, they can be paid by cash or check. Once paid, they're basically gone: what a clear-cut way of dealing with life!

Being a "sinner" is different, since that, by theological definition, is a permanent existential state. *Ora pro nobis peccatoribus* ... But the vague appellation of "sinner," as opposed to the more precise "murderer," "adulterer," "liar," sits lightly on one's shoulders. And since everyone is a sinner, that doesn't tell us very much. Just as sins can be forgiven and so done away with, sinners can be saved. One thinks of the famous epitaph of the fallen soldier in the English Civil War, "Betwixt the stirrup and the ground,/ Mercy I asked, and mercy found." That is, a person's entire life can be transformed in a millisecond, with all the unpleasant, ugly, destructive features miraculously removed. Time can be overcome, something pessimism knows is impossible.

Thus sin, which has often been used to weigh people down, to literally depress them, turns out, upon closer inspection, to be a flimsily built concept, too fanciful, uncritical, and narrow, to be of much use. It demeans humans without enlightening them. *Che peccato*, as the Italians say, what a sin (shame)! Redemption, if it existed, and if it only meant redemption from sin, would never be enough.

Some otherwise illuminating schools of thought have likewise gone overboard with unbalanced pessimism. Buddhism's first Noble Truth, that all things are *dukkha*, or suffering, like many other sweeping absolutes invented by men, is clearly excessive. No doubt there's much truth to it; no doubt it has a solid, peremptory, let's-get-down-to-the-nitty-gritty flavor to it; but it's nonetheless wrong. Not *all* grapes are sour; not *all* sweet drinks leave a bitter aftertaste. Just because life as a whole is futile (as pessimism believes) that doesn't mean it doesn't have a lot of riveting side-shows. Buddhism saves its adherents from many sorts of addictions, but only at the cost of diminished vitality (a price that may be worth paying, for some people at any rate). Such philosophical approaches, like Alcoholics Anonymous, undoubtedly "work," but teetotalism isn't for everyone.

Similarly, Schopenhauer achieves a brilliant clarity by declaring that, "Day by day it will get worse—until the worst of all arrives." This sort of oversimplification absolutizes the downward flow of old age, as only a man without children or grandchildren could have done. What goads the pessimistic exaggerators into their overkill is probably a response to the foggy-mindedness, hypocrisy, and lies spouted by the "children of this world," who seem to prefer anything to harsh reality. (Or are the pessimists unconsciously afraid of life's delectable lures?)

Another good example of silly pessimism, is T.S. Eliot's *The Waste Land* (1928), with its matchless pictures of urban desolation, conveniently unrelieved by pictures of an even more desolating past. Yes, London in the 1920s was polluted, but not as badly as it had been in the 19th century. Yes, life was miserable, and sex was alienated for many Londoners; but there was far more freedom and opportunity for ordinary people then than in earlier days. There was even good jazz, despite the inanity of Eliot's "Shakes-pe-herian rag." But then, if the unchurched modern urbanites could somehow manage to find a reasonably good life, that would put Christianity in a rather different light. Believers seem to be obsessed with the idea that unbelievers are miserable.

At the other end of the philosophical spectrum, Albert Camus wrote in *The Myth of Sisyphus* (1942) that *the* issue for "modern man" was whether or not to commit suicide. That may be true in some airy theoretical realm; but to this day only a tiny minority of people (consciously) commit suicide. This may prove their philosophical inconsistency, their cowardice or immaturity; but it also clearly demonstrates nature's success at keeping her children in the game. No pessimistic account of life can (or wishes to) ignore its phenomenally addictive grip on the vast majority of its participants. This explains, among other things, the familiar paradox that even believers with intense convictions about the splendor of the afterlife take all the usual precautions to remain firmly ensconced in the Here and Now. No surprise, of course, but any school of philosophy that blinks all the powerful enticements to remain alive will ever amount to much.

So pessimism has to be rescued from the hands of the silly pessimists. Given its pragmatic origins, sensible pessimism has to keep making pragmatic and fallible calculations about the world around us. Its negative foundations, unfortunately, are doubtless secure, though not because of some ancient, never re-examined prejudice. The evidence keeps coming in, and has to be constantly updated. In the 1980s, for instance, a diagnosis of AIDS was an automatic death sentence. Now, at least for American with good health care plans, it no longer is; and Magic Johnson may live to be 100 (Of course, this only gives an added poignancy to stories from that time—and reports from the vast regions of the world with next to no modern medicine.) So, we needn't be vexed by silly pessimism—every great idea has its third-rate imitators.

18

WHO NEEDS ALL THIS STUFF:
PESSIMISM VS. CREATION

Everyone who has religious ideas must have been puzzled by
what we may call the irrelevancy of creation to his religion. We
find ourselves lodged in a vast theatre, in which a ceaseless
action, a perpetual shifting of scenes, and unresting life, is going
forward; and that life seems physical, unmoral, having no relation
to what our souls tell us to be great and good, to what religion
says is the design of all things. Especially when we see any new
objects or scenes, or countries, we feel this. Look at a great
tropical plant, with large leaves stretching everywhere, and great
stalks branching out on all sides; with a big beetle on a leaf, and
a humming-bird on a branch, and an ugly lizard just below. What
has such an object to do with *us*—with anything we can conceive,
or hope, or imagine? What *could* it be created for, if creation has
a moral end and object? Or go into a gravel-pit, or stone-quarry;
you see there a vast accumulation of dull matter, yellow or gray,
and you ask, involuntarily and of necessity, why is all this waste
and irrelevant production, as it would seem, of material? Can
anything seem more stupid than a big stone *as* a big stone, than
gravel for gravel's sake? What is the use of such cumbrous,
inexpressive objects in a world where there are minds to be filled,
and imaginations to be aroused, and souls to be saved?

—Walter Bagehot, "The Ignorance of Man" (1862)

I t's (vaguely) interesting that not one in a hundred people know what
samaras are, though everyone has seen them: those little wing-shaped,
one-seeded fruits of elms, ash, or maple that come pouring out of the trees

in spring, briefly flooding the streets and sidewalks until (in almost all cases) they dry up, get swept away and disappear. This, of course, is the fate of most seeds that aren't carefully planted and cultivated. It's also the case, more poignantly perhaps for humans, with sperm, which males produce by the trillions and then scatter, almost always unproductively, in all sorts of places, or never even get around to ejaculating, much less fertilizing ova with.

Redundancy is one of the keys to nature. It's pleasant when it comes in the form of having an extra copy of an organ that we really need, as with eyes, lungs, kidneys, ovaries and testicles, etc. But when we see the sheer "waste" and excess, the ridiculous proliferation of raw material throughout the universe, the pessimistic implications are clear. It's a sign of the randomness and sloppiness of the cosmos.

Quite apart from the miniscule biosphere we inhabit, what's the use (for us? for anybody? for anything?) of all the incalculable, boring (dare one say?) mass of *stuff* out there? We spend so much of our time in the humanly structured and purposeful (however aesthetically hideous) world of city streets and buildings, where endless civic, commercial, and electronic grids intersect and overlap, that we barely notice the "eternal silence of those infinite spaces." As Nietzsche observed in *The Gay Science*, 109: "*Let us be on guard*!—Let us be in guard against thinking that the universe is a living being? Whither is it supposed to expand? What is it supposed to feed on? How could it grow and multiply?... Let us be on guard against believing the universe is a machine: it was certainly not built with any goal in mind. We do it far too high an honor with the world 'machine'." We may be tempted to humanize everything, but that's a temptation we have to resist, for the sake of honesty. One can only laugh at the declaration by the United Nations in 1967 that outer space was "the province of all man-kind"—the last frontier of imperialistic colonization, as it were. Only in this case even the most stalwart and ferocious of the modern-day Pizarros will have to limit his incursions to fantasies on pictures sent back by the Hubble telescope.

One of the moist revealing examples of this penchant is the absence of all, or almost all, non-human life (and natural entities of any sort) from Christian and Muslim images of the afterlife. The biblical doctrine of creation is based on the delirious notion that everything in the cosmos was put there to be dominated and exploited by humans. Of course, this view received a couple of body-blows when the actual size and age of the universe began to be understood. If humans were the be-all and end-all (and if God was, in the final analysis, just a sort of supremely glorified Man), then why those vast incalculable stretches of time and space without any trace of humanity? Why bother making dinosaurs (trilobites, ammonites, etc.) and having them hang around for tens of millions of years, only to let them go extinct, like 99% of all species? What need is there, strictly speaking, for lichens and sloths and okapis, for all the snow and ice in Antarctica, the sand in the Sahara, the empty real estate in Greenland (not to mention unreachable galaxies, supernovae, comets, and so forth), especially when there'll be no one to see them? The idea that a single atom on top of Mount Everest could think of itself not just as the "summit of creation," but as the supreme goal toward which everything else was oriented, takes the cake for maniacal narcissism. Religious "teleologists," of the sort parodied in Voltaire's Pangloss, like to claim that everything in the universe was somehow put there for our benefit. That absurd pretension might almost be justified by extending "benefit" to mean "good to study" (or at least "pleasant to think about"). But that won't work, either: there's entirely too much stuff, most of it shapeless, to grasp, much less dream of.

Pessimism insists on facing the music (that is, the cacophony of the universe), if only to appreciate better the bits of melody that *are* accidentally out there or that we create or imagine. It reminds us that, as Nietzsche would say, there are an infinite number of perspectives, none of them supreme or ultimate. It forbids us from sentimentally exalting happenstance (in any given "mountain greenery" we, and not God, "paint the scenery"), from seeking or pretending to have found permanence. It bites the bullet, or the samaras (not very tasty, by the way).

Alternately, one might say, how fortunate we are that the great bulk of the universe is, as far as we can tell, just blah-blah-blah, incalculable stretches of lifeless empty space, rocks, dust, sand, gases, and so on (in any event no humans, even if they traveled at the speed of light, could reach and touch more than a tiny chunk of it). It's likely as awful as recent photos of Titan, Saturn's gigantic satellite, reveal: a hideous mass of smog, dirt, and "rivers" of frozen methane, with no life in sight. Yecch. Not to mention the billions of years of "lost" time before we ever appeared, or the eternity that will follow our vanishing. How frustrated we would feel if the cosmos consisted of an endless string of, so to speak, national-park-quality gems, whose beauties we would never get around to seeing, much less savoring? In a harsh burst of elitism, Voltaire once wrote that, "The world is full of people who aren't worth talking to." The key to the manageability of life may be the ineluctable fact that, quite apart from the abysses of utterly boring intergalactic space, most people aren't worth talking to, most books not worth reading, most streets not worth walking down, most sights not worth seeing, most facts not worth knowing, most objects not worth having. Flick on your TV, and the odds are that what comes in will be garbage. And that, unlike the wastelands of outer space, had a great deal of planning and so-called intelligence behind it. So we're off the hook.

In any case, not to worry: The world, even in its ravaged state, has far more beauty, human and otherwise, old and new, of every sort and shape, than any one person could ever get to the end of—at least until we destroy the planet completely. Pessimism is simply here to remind us not to sentimentalize over that beauty, to recognize how rare it is, and to enjoy it while it lasts. Treasure the one samara in a million that hits pay dirt and blossoms.

19

DON'T TELL ME HOW IT ENDS
ESCHATOLOGICAL PESSIMISM

> That man is the product of causes which had no prevision of the
> end they were achieving; that his origin, his growth, his hopes
> and fears, his loves and his beliefs, are but the outcome of
> accidental collocations of atoms; that no fire, no heroism, no
> intensity of thought and feeling can preserve an individual life
> beyond the grave, that all the labours of all the ages, all the
> devotion, all the inspiration, all the noonday brightness of human
> genius are destined to extinction in the vast death of the solar
> system, and that the whole temple of man's achievement must
> inevitably be buried beneath the debris of a universe in ruins—all
> these things, if not quite beyond dispute, are yet so nearly certain
> that no philosophy which rejects them can hope to stand.

—Bertrand Russell, *Mysticism and Logic* (1947)

Ever since the dawn of the nuclear age there's been a flood of (a boom
in?) apocalyptic scenarios about the end of life on earth. And with the
growth of the ecology movement has come a spate of warnings about what
might happen if humanity carried—or, more likely, once it has carried—its
current destructive behavior to the point of self-annihilation. Since these
visions, unlike the ones in the Book of Revelation, are based—for the most
part—on hard science rather than resentful pious fantasy, they can't be
simply scoffed at.

On the other hand, there's always something fundamentally unreal
about such speculations. This or that horror or all of them together MIGHT
occur in a given order at a given pace, but surely not in *my* lifetime. In any

case, it's hard to feel their hot breath on our necks, except in some simplistic disaster movie; and in the meantime we have bills to pay and children to drop off at school.

Jonathan Swift, whose pessimistic credentials are not in doubt, satirized such end-of-the-world anxiety in the form of the hyper-rational Laputans. As Gulliver reports:

> These people are under continual disquietudes, never enjoying a minute's peace of mind; and their disturbances proceed from causes which very little affect the rest of mortals. Their apprehensions arise from several changes they dread in the celestial bodies. For instance that the earth, by the continual approaches of the sun towards it, must in course of time be absorbed or swallowed up. That the face of the sun will by degrees be encrusted with its own effluvia, and give no more light to the world. That the earth very narrowly escaped a brush from the tail of the last comet, which would have infallibly reduced it to ashes.

Of course, change "last comet" to "giant meteorite," and the stakes get higher; but the point is obvious. As Jesus said, probably echoing an old Jewish proverb, sufficient for the day is the evil thereof (Mt. 6.34).

Still, while actively worrying about our quotidian troubles, it's tempting to sneak a peek at the end of the world (or the biosphere), the solar system, the cosmos, whatever, even if we can do so only by extrapolation. This is the sort of thing our obsessively inquiring minds want to know. Even though we have to leave before the movie ends, a glimpse of the final frame might, if nothing else, help to evaluate the judgments we've made of the picture so far.

It took a long time before believers (honest, educated ones at least) finally gave up on the argument from design. But even if that meant admitting the existence of all sorts of flaws in the universe, it was hard not to view our world as a sort of masterpiece (though what could it be compared with?), and, at the very least, as a single object of discourse (universe). More than a century ago William James, an ex-Christian who tried to give religion every possible break, penned a telling footnote to *The Varieties of Religious Experience* (1902):

> When one views the world with no definite theological bias one way or the other, one sees that order and disorder as we now recognize them are purely human inventions. We are interested in certain types of arrangement, useful, aesthetic, or moral,—so interested that whenever we find them realized, the fact emphatically rivets our attention. The result is that

we work over the contents of the world selectively. It is overflowing with disorderly arrangements from our point of view, but order is the only thing we care for and look at, and by choosing, one can always find some sort of orderly arrangement in the midst of any chaos... . There are in reality infinitely more things "unadapted" to each other in this world than there are things "adapted"; infinitely more things with irregular relations than with regular relations between them.

We may know all *that*—and with a little serious reflection the idea becomes more or less axiomatic—but it still flies in the face of "common sense" and spontaneous feeling. A conscious person can't actually imagine himself or herself as completely *gone*; and imagining a human-less, lifeless, "unadapted" world likewise challenges the mind. But surely the earth—unless we blow it up first—will some day freeze when the sun is extinguished; and our "story" will have neither tellers nor listeners ever again. Disorder will overcome order. Given the scenario sketched out by Bertrand Russell in *Mysticism and Logic*, as ultimately inevitable as it is temporally remote, one might be tempted to call the totality of human (and animal and floral and mineral) events "much ado about nothing." And that would be an unimpeachably pessimistic formula.

Knowing how things terrestrial will, in all likelihood, end provides perspective, a bold black frame against which to set such joys and pleasures as can be found in the meantime. Moses on Mt. Nebo presumably felt some satisfaction in scanning Eretz Israel from afar, even though he'd never enter it; and Martin Luther King, Jr. shared this bittersweet Mosaic enjoyment in his vision of a better world just before he was shot. But how do such hopeful speculations (and similar utopian dreams) measure against the ultimate long run, when we will all, we know, be dead? Consider what Arthur James Balfour, better known nowadays for the part he played in the founding of the state of Israel, wrote about the dissolution of the whole world in *The Foundations of Belief* (1895):

> The energies of our system will decay, the glory of the sun will be dimmed, and the earth, tideless and inert, will no longer tolerate the race which has for a moment disturbed its solitude. Man will go down into the pit, and all his thoughts will perish. The uneasy consciousness which has in this obscure corner has for a brief space broken the contented silence of the universe, will be at rest. Matter will know itself no longer. 'Imperishable monuments' and 'immortal deeds,' death itself, and love stronger than death, will be as if they had not been. Nor will anything that is, be better or worse for all that the labor, genius, devotion, and suffering of man may

have striven through countless ages to effect. (quoted in William James, *Pragmatism and Other Writings*).

In passing, one can't but notice how Balfour borrows scriptural cadences to sound the notes of solemnity and finality that so powerfully mark this passage. Such a desolating scene seems to call for verses from the Book of Uncreation. Perhaps we'd be better off not knowing about this cosmic dead-end; but after a bit of reflection on basic science we can't help realizing the truth of Russell and Balfour's words. Once we know it, we can't forget it; and we have to deal with it.

Well, in fact, as the behavior of our fellow humans, educated or otherwise, constantly shows us, we *don't* have to deal with it. But thoughtful people will be inclined to, and for them pessimism is ready and waiting with its rational, useful, if not exactly exhilarating world-picture. If nothing else, pessimism can provide us with a limitless supply of humility. We now know far better than King David ever did, that "We are strangers ... and sojourners, as all our fathers were; our days on earth are like a shadow, and there is no abiding" (1 Chr. 29.15). A worthy prelude to the words of his son Solomon—if one wishes to think anything attributed to any speaker in the Bible was ever actually spoken by that person— "Then I considered all that my hands had done and the toil I had spent in doing it, and behold, all was vanity and a striving after wind, and there was nothing to be gained under the sun" (Eccl. 1.11). As usual, when you want a powerful dose of pessimism, nothing beats the Bible.

The bottom line here seems to be: lifeless matter will go on forever and forever, in some form or other, because it has no place to go outside the universe. Whatever cosmic entropy means, the phrase suggests dull, disorganized piles of stuff—which won't matter if there's no one around to complain about how ugly it looks. Long, long before that happens we will all have turned to dust (which might be very good news for any life form that happened to outlive us), because no species is forever. Since no one reading, much less the person writing, this will be there to witness even the beginning of our disappearance, the whole point might be moot. But if we want to bet on likely scenarios, the pessimists have got one.

20

EPILOGUE:
THE JOY OF PESSIMISM

Ah, make the most of what we may yet spend,
Before we too into the Dust descend;
  Dust unto Dust, and under Dust to lie,
Sans Wine, sans Song , sans Singer, and–sans End!

—*The Rubáiyát of Omar Khayyam,*
24, tr. Edward Fitzgerald

In a footnote to *Civilization and Its Discontents* Freud says that the educational system of his day was sending young people out on the polar expedition of life with the sort of summer clothing and maps better suited for a romp around the lakes of Northern Italy. In this sense, a training in pessimism provides its adherents with the proper boots, wool socks, layered garments, parka, and so forth needed to resist, and at times positively enjoy, the frosty weather outside.

And while out on the "trail," one small volume that thoughtful travelers might bring along is *The Rubáiyát of Omar Khayyam* in Edward Fitzgerald's exquisitely plangent rendition. The message echoes the work of Lucretius, Horace, and the Epicurean tradition in general; but, thanks to Fitzgerald, it's more pungent and accessible. (No one has ever translated Horace well.)

48

A Moment's Halt—a momentary taste
Of BEING from the Well amid the Waste
And Lo!—the phantom Caravan has reached
The NOTHING it set out from—Oh, make haste!

Still, Fitzgerald's version, apart from being extremely free and fanciful, skips many of the original quatrains, for which we have to shop around in less inspired, but fuller translations, such as E.H. Whinfield's (1917):

387

Since all man's business in this world of woe
Is sorrow's pangs to tell and grief to know,
Happy are they that never come at all,
And they that, having come, the soonest go.

There it is again, for the last time, the theme of "better than both," the outrageous notion that the luckiest humans are the ones who never made it out of the womb. But, for all the negativity that seems to imply, pessimism, as this book has tried to show, needn't mean depression: just a sensible way of playing the cards we've been dealt. We're bound to lose the game in the end, and if that distresses you overmuch, you can always bail out by suicide. (But it might be worth recalling that Albert Camus, who compared the human condition to Sisyphus' continuously pushing a heavy rock up a hill in Hades, maintained that we have to imagine Sisyphus happy: It's *his* rock; it's *his* hill; it's *his* fate.)

The logical consequence of pessimism is not desperation but careful economizing of pleasure. Since the world is as the pessimists describe it, eat, drink, and be merry (all in moderation, if possible). That, of course, is the conclusion of the arch-pessimist, and proto-Khayyam, Ecclesiastes. "Enjoy life with the wife whom you love, all thee days of your vain life which he has given you under the sun, because that is your portion in life and in your toil at which you toil under the sun" (Eccl. 9.9). And, as the man reputed to be both the wisest, wealthiest, and most fortunate of men, Solomon should know. (For reasons the Bible never bothers to explain, David—who was more spontaneously devout and pious than Solomon— had to endure a much harder life, as a punishment for his sins. He had to endure the death of his infant son by Bathsheba, the rape of his daughter

Tamar by his son Amnon, the murder of Amnon by his adored son Absalom, the rebellion and death of Absalom, along with many other afflictions. Solomon, by contrast, through a gross idolater in his old age (suckered into paganism by the seven hundred wives and three hundred concubines in his harem), got off scot-free—which might, ironically, account for Ecclesiastes' conviction that life isn't fair.

Pessimism deflates doomed expectations, and thus spares its adherents the inevitable let-downs caused by false accounts of life, such as religious ones. It prepares us for the worst, thus assuring us a certain lift when we encounter anything better than that. As Thomas Carlyle pontifically proclaimed in *Sartor Resartus* (1833-34), "So true is it, what I then say, that *the Fraction of Life can be increased in value not so much by increasing your Numerator as by lessening the Denominator.* Nay, unless my Algebra deceive me, *Unity* itself divided by *Zero* will give *Infinity.* Make thy claim of wages a zero, then; thou hast the world under thy feet." Well, you can't argue with that. Pessimism, the sober calculating of the odds by the best lights we have, is wiser than hedonism, wiser than hope, and certainly wiser than the dumbest, most naïve and most (consciously or otherwise) self-deceiving of all philosophies: optimism.

ABOUT THE AUTHOR

Born in Brooklyn, Peter Heinegg was educated at Fordham University, Columbia, and Harvard (Ph.D., Comparative Literature). He is a professor of English at Union College, Schenectady, N.Y. He has translated some fifty books on philosophy and religion from German, French, Italian, and Russian; and is the author of *Mortalism: Readings on the Meaning of Life* (Prometheus Press), along with numerous essays and book reviews.